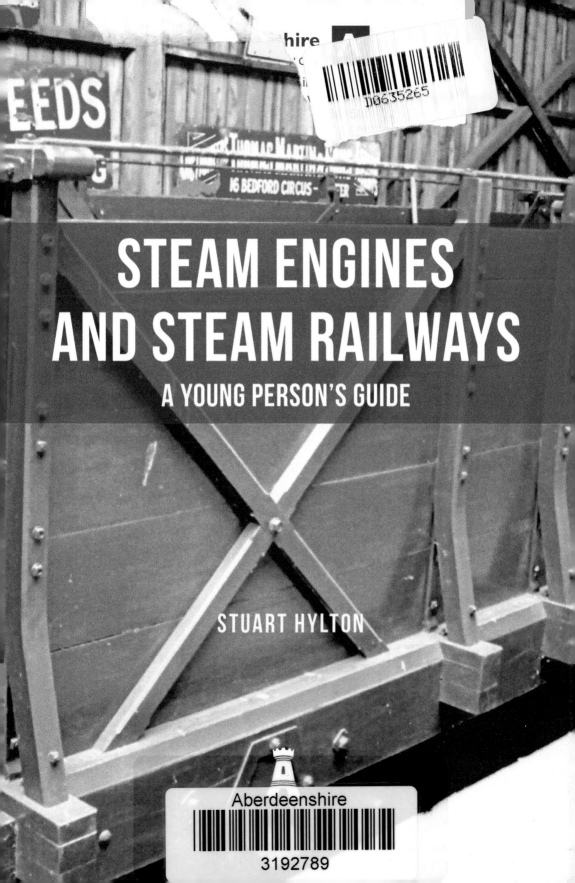

STEAM ENGINES AND STEAM RAILWAYS

A YOUNG PERSON'S GUIDE

STUART HYLTON

First published 2016

Amberley Publishing
The Hill, Stroud
Gloucestershire, GL5 4EP

www.amberley-books.com

Copyright © Stuart Hylton, 2016

The right of Stuart Hylton to be identified as the
Author of this work has been asserted in accordance
with the Copyrights, Designs and Patents Act 1988.

ISBN 978 1 4456 5668 7 (print)
ISBN 978 1 4456 5669 4 (ebook)

British Library Cataloguing in Publication Data.
A catalogue record for this book is available from the
British Library.

Typesetting by Amberley Publishing.
Printed in the UK.

CONTENTS

INTRODUCTION

For me, steam railways bring back memories of my own childhood. I used to go to Slough station to watch the Great Western steam expresses thunder past on their way to Bristol or the seaside resorts of Devon and Cornwall. For you, born after the age of steam, the steam railways are a window into the past. They can tell you a lot about how people lived in the past 200 years, and how their lives changed as a result of the railway revolution.

As for the railway locomotives themselves, they are far more like living creatures than the diesel and electric trains that replaced them. Thomas Grey, seeing an early locomotive in 1820, described it as a 'walking horse', and the steam that it puffed out being like the breath of an animal.

What I try to do in this book is to give you an introduction to the world of the steam railway: how a locomotive works; how to drive one; the history of steam railways, from their start to their last days with British Rail; how they changed the world; how the railways are kept safe; and a host of information about things you might see when you visit some of Britain's many steam railways.

For a long time in the old steam railway days, men got to do the best jobs. Women were not allowed to do exciting things like driving the locomotives. This has all changed now, and women can do anything to do with railways. You can see plenty of women drivers on British Rail. So far it is mainly men who get involved with the historic steam railways, but that is slowly changing. So if, in my book, I say 'he' can do something connected with steam railways, what I really mean is 'he or she'. I hope that I will have some female readers, and that some of them will be part of that change.

Some railway words

You might find it useful to understand some railway words from the start.

Gauge is the distance between the two rails. On our modern main-line railways, that distance is 4 feet, 8.5 inches (about 144 centimetres) but there are many other gauges. A locomotive built to one gauge will not run on a different gauge of track. The **loading gauge** describes the maximum size of any train that can safely pass along a section of track without hitting anything.

A **steam engine** means any machine that uses steam power to make it work. It could be a machine that pumps water out of a mine, a machine inside a building that pulls trucks along on the end of ropes, or a moving steam machine that goes along a railway or road.

A **steam locomotive** is a moving steam engine. The ones we are mainly interested in in this book run on rails, but it could also run on the roads.

A **steam train** is a locomotive *and* the trucks or carriages it pulls. A locomotive on its own, without any carriages or trucks, is not a train.

A **bogie** is a frame with suspension, axles and wheels attached. Railway vehicles (locomotives, carriages or trucks) are mounted on them. They can turn independently of the vehicle, and they carry part of the weight of the vehicle and help it stay safely on the track.

Third rail. This is a book about steam railways, but I do talk about electric trains as well. There are two types of electric train. One gets its power from electric cables hung above the train. The other – known as third rail – gets its power from an extra rail that sits next to the two main rails. The main thing you need to know about the third rail is to keep well away from it!

A number of other railway words are explained as we go.

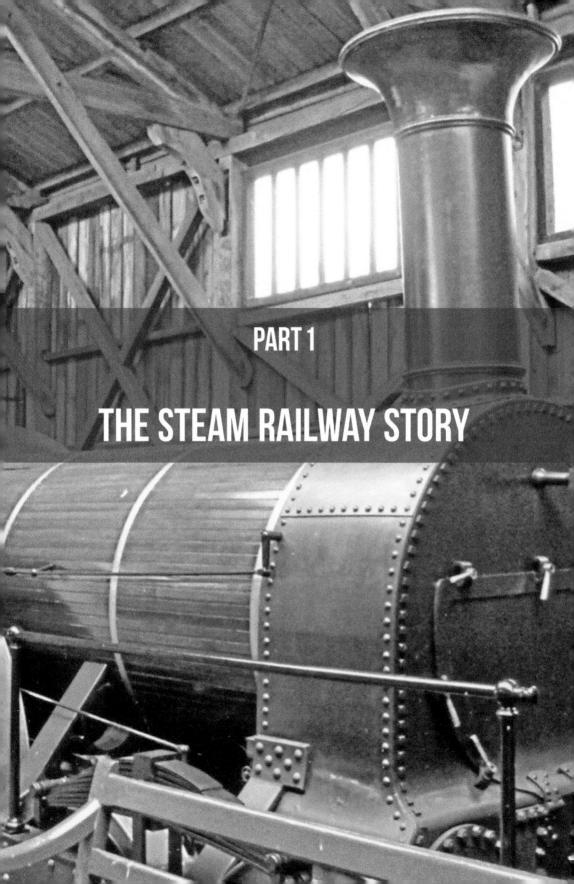

PART 1

THE STEAM RAILWAY STORY

CHAPTER 1

THE FIRST RAILWAYS

Before the steam railways

Railways and steam engines both existed for hundreds of years before the first steam-powered railway was built. The very first railways were built by the ancient Babylonians in about 2245 BC. Greeks and Romans also had a kind of railway over 2,000 years ago. They used stones with grooves cut in them to help steer wagons. They all had a gauge of about 5 feet – roughly the gauge George Stephenson chose for his railways, 2000 years later. About a thousand years after the ancient Romans, in about 1350, a picture of an early railway was shown in the stained glass window of a church in Germany. In England, from the time of the first Queen Elizabeth, coal-mine owners were using railways to carry their coal from the mines to the river, where it could be loaded onto boats. All of the earliest railways were used for moving goods, not people.

Why did they use railways? Because it was much easier to move wagons along smooth rails than it was to pull them over rough or muddy ground. A horse can pull a truck weighing about a ton along a road. That same horse could pull wagons weighing up to 40 tons along a railway.

But these railways had two important differences to modern ones. First, the rails were made of wood, not metal. This meant that they soon wore out or broke, and had to be replaced. Then someone had the idea of fixing metal strips along the top of the wooden rails. This made them last a little longer. Finally, in Coalbrookdale in 1767, they made rails completely out of iron. This was better still, but they still would not be able to support a very heavy steam locomotive. Only when they found a cheap way of making steel were the rails strong enough for the heaviest locomotives. The second difference was that these early railways did not have any steam engines to move the trucks. Instead, they used men, horses or other animals to pull them, or simply let the trucks roll downhill by themselves.

The first public railway to be approved by Parliament was the Leeds & Middleton Wagonway in 1758. It needed an Act of Parliament to enable the company to buy the land it needed for the railway. Before this, railways were built on the railway-builder's own land. Another one, the Surrey Iron Railway between Croydon and Wandsworth (now parts of London), opened in 1803. By the start of the nineteenth century, there were, by some estimates, about 1,500 miles of railway in Britain. Many of them were in the mining areas of north-east England. Some of them were built instead of digging an expensive canal to carry goods. However, none of these carried passengers until the Oystermouth Railway, between Swansea and Mumbles in Wales, opened in 1807. But the carriages on that railway were still pulled by horses.

The first steam engines

The first man to realise that steam could be used to move things was called Hero of Alexandria. He was an inventor who lived in Egypt about 2,000 years ago. He made a toy – a metal ball filled with water, fixed onto a stand. When you heated the ball, it would make steam come out of two little bent tubes, fixed to the ball. This would make the ball go round and round. Sadly for him, no one could think of a use for his toy, and it was forgotten about for over a thousand years.

The first real use of steam came in 1698. By this time, men were digging deep mines to get coal and iron ore from under the ground. But many of these mines were flooded, and a way was needed to get the water out of the mine. Thomas Savery invented a steam pump that would suck the water out. It worked, but it was slow. Nor was it very safe because, in those days, no one knew how to make a machine that could hold steam under pressure. (The section of the book showing how a steam engine works explains about pressure.) One of Savery's engines exploded in about 1705, and most people gave up on them after that.

Another inventor, Thomas Newcomen, built an improved machine (called an *atmospheric engine*) in 1712. This could suck more water from deeper mines, and did not use dangerous high-pressure steam. But it was still very slow, heavy and used a lot of coal for the amount of water it sucked out. Even so, about 100 of his engines were in use in England by 1735, and some improvements were made to them by others during the eighteenth century.

The next big improvements were made by a Scotsman, James Watt. He made many changes to the Newcomen machine but, in 1765, the tools and the skilled workmen needed to build steam engines to his exact designs still did not exist. His machines still could not use high-pressure steam, and he stopped anyone else from trying to make high-pressure machines. Watt drew up a design for a steam carriage, but never built one. His engines were still too heavy and slow to fit into any kind of moving machine. Watt could not stop people in America from making new types of steam engines. In 1788, an American called John Fitch built a steamboat that ran along the Delaware River and, by the early 1800s, a number of steamboats were working on American rivers.

By the end of the eighteenth century, Watt's *patents* (the laws that he used to stop others in England copying his ideas and making an improved engine) had run out. People were free to experiment, and a man from Cornwall, Richard Trevithick, got his own patent for a steam-powered carriage to run on the roads. He built it, but nobody was interested in using it.

About this time, two businessmen in Wales made bets with each other about whether a steam locomotive running on rails was possible. Their answer came on 21 February 1804. Richard Trevithick had built another self-propelled steam carriage (or *locomotive*). This one was designed to run on rails. It was brought to the Penydarren Iron Works at Merthyr Tydfil, South Wales, to settle the bet. It pulled wagons weighing ten tons along a 9.5-mile track. It completed the journey and was the first ever steam railway trip. The local newspaper reported the journey and said it was very important.

Sadly, the engine was too heavy for the rails they had at that time, and kept breaking them. They soon stopped using the locomotive, took its wheels off and used the steam it made to power a hammer. Trevithick went on to build the first passenger-carrying steam locomotive, called *Catch Me Who Can*, in 1808. He gave rides on it in London, as a kind of fairground novelty. But again, no one thought that it could be a practical way of travelling.

Catch Me Who Can, the world's first passenger-carrying steam locomotive. Built in 1808 by Richard Trevithick, it gave novelty rides on a circular track in London, but no one was interested in developing it as a serious way of travelling. This replica lives at Bridgnorth, on the Severn Valley Railway.

Over the next twenty years, a few more people tried using steam locomotives. One of the most famous of these was William Blackett, who owned the Wylam coal mine near Newcastle. In about 1813–14 he ordered two steam engines, which were named *Puffing Billy* and *Wylam Dilly*. These were successful, and *Puffing Billy* remained in use until 1862. You can see them today – Billy is in the Science Museum in London and Dilly is in the Royal Museum in Edinburgh. They are the oldest surviving steam locomotives in the world. A modern copy of *Puffing Billy* runs at the Beamish open-air museum in Durham.

Near to Wylam was another coal mine, Killingworth, where a man had the job of looking after their stationary steam engines. His name was George Stephenson and, in 1814, he built his first steam locomotive, which was called *Blucher* after an army commander from Prussia. George would become one of the most famous people in the history of railways.

The first public steam railways

The Stockton & Darlington Railway

Before the railway came, an 80-lb (36 kilogram) bag of coal would cost you 2½ old pence if you bought it at the coal mine near the town of Bishop Auckland. By the time that same coal reached Darlington, 12 miles away, the price had gone up to 8 old pence. Much of this increase was due to the cost of delivering it, which was by pack horses. The mine-owners and the people buying coal both wanted to find a way of reducing that cost.

In 1810 a leading canal builder, John Rennie, was brought in to look at a possible canal, or a tramway (an early type of railway) to transport this coal more cheaply. He suggested a canal, but it did not get built, since the country was at war at the time and nobody wanted to pay for it. The idea reappeared in 1818, this time in the form of a horse-drawn railway. It was decided to apply to Parliament for permission to build it.

But it was not easy getting the first railways built. Many landowners did not want railways running across their land. They would even try and stop the railway company coming onto their land to plan the route. Sometimes this would become violent. In some cases there were even battles, with large numbers of railway workers fighting with large numbers of the landowner's men. There were no violent battles over this particular railway, which became known as the Stockton & Darlington Railway, but it was opposed by many important landowners along the route. Some of them were making a lot of money from people using horses to transport things, even though that took longer. One – the Earl of Darlington – opposed the railway because it might get in the way of his foxhunting! Between them, they managed to get the first railway plan rejected. Also, the lawmakers in London crossed out any mention of 'locomotives' in the plans, because many of them did not even know what a locomotive was!

A second plan for the railway was approved in 1821, but it was still not clear how the railway would work – they talked about it being powered by 'men, horses or otherwise'. But the man now chosen to build the railway was George Stephenson, who we heard about earlier. He was a great supporter of steam locomotives. Only when they had to go back to Parliament to agree some changes to the route was the idea of passengers being transported by steam locomotives approved.

Building the railway was not simple. Along the route it needed an embankment 48 feet high, the crossing of a swamp called Myers Flat and a bridge over the River Skerne that was almost 40 feet wide and 30 feet above the river. But the railway was completed and opened in September 1825.

The Stockton & Darlington Railway was not really the first modern railway. It had several important differences to the ones we know today. The original idea had been that the railway company would provide just the rails, and people who wanted to use it would have to provide their own locomotives and trucks. So anyone could use the railway, no matter how good or bad their wagons were, or whether they had steam engines or horses to pull them.

The railway only had a single track, shared by trains going in both directions, with occasional places for trains to pass each other. There were lots of fights about who should go first. There was no timetable. Parts of it relied on stationary steam engines to pull the trains. The horse-drawn carriages used to get in the way of the steam engines when the steam engines were working properly. But when the steam engines broke down,

This locomotive was used in building the Liverpool & Manchester Railway in 1828/29. It looks very much like *Locomotion No. 1*, the engine that ran on the Stockton & Darlington Railway. It was already obsolete compared with *Rocket*, which was also built about this time.

they held up the horse-drawn carriages. The railway company soon had to stop just anyone using the tracks, and run all the trains themselves.

However, despite its problems, the railway made a great difference to people's lives. The price of coal in Stockton, which used to be 18 shillings a ton, fell to 8 shillings and 6 pence in old money.

The Liverpool & Manchester Railway

The title of the first modern railway really belongs to the one opened in 1830 between the port of Liverpool and the large industrial town of Manchester. Manchester was the world's greatest centre for making cotton cloth. The raw cotton used to arrive in the docks at Liverpool and was delivered to Manchester by canal. But the delivery was very slow and very expensive. It sometimes took longer for the raw cotton to travel the few miles from Liverpool to Manchester than it did to bring it all the way from America. Businessmen in both towns were unhappy about this, and looked for a better way of doing it. They decided on a railway.

Once again, lots of people were opposed to the idea, such as the canal owners, stagecoach and turnpike road operators, who could see the railway taking their business. Many wealthy people had shares in the canals. Several rich landowners also lived on the route planned for the railway. They did not want it to come anywhere near their private estates. They did their best to stop the railway workers coming on their land to look at the route. Lord Sefton said he would send a small army of 100 men to keep them out. When the railway people tried to sneak into the estate by night to do their surveys, another landowner, Robert Bradshaw, sent his men to fire guns to scare them off.

The man chosen to design and build the railway was, once again, George Stephenson. But he had little training in designing a railway and had a lot of other work to do. This, and the difficulty of getting onto the route to look at it because of the people who didn't want the railway, meant that Stephenson got some of his measurements badly wrong. When his proposals came before Parliament, his opponents were able to make a fool of him. His plan was thrown out and Stephenson lost his job.

A new firm of expert surveyors, George and John Rennie, got the job of revising the scheme for a second application. They managed to deal with many of the problems, and steered the railway away from some of its biggest opponents' land. Even more important, the railway promoters managed to get one of the main canal owners – the Marquis of Stafford – to invest £100,000 in the railway scheme. The second application was approved by Parliament in May, 1826.

By this time, the Stockton & Darlington Railway had opened and was a success. George Stephenson was back in favour. He was reappointed to build the Liverpool & Manchester Railway. Once again there were problems to deal with. Perhaps the biggest was an area called Chat Moss. This used to be a lake, but had become a watery swamp, where men and horses could disappear without trace into the mud. Nobody believed Chat Moss could support the weight of a railway – nobody except George Stephenson. He poured huge amounts of earth and other material into the Moss until he had a solid route for the railway to run along.

Parliament's permission for the railway had all sorts of limits attached to it. One of the oddest was that, at first, steam locomotives were not allowed into either Manchester or Liverpool, because people were so frightened of them. The railway company had to go back to Parliament to be allowed to extend their railway into Manchester.

All sorts of wild stories were spread by their opponents about the harm steam locomotives would do. According to them, the locomotive would forever be crashing, exploding or setting fire to the countryside; their passengers would not be able to breath, due to going too fast, and would die; horses, pheasants and foxes would become extinct and cows would stop grazing; hens would stop laying eggs and birds would die when they flew through the smoke.

At first, it was not even certain that this railway would use steam locomotives – some of the railway's managers preferred stationary steam engines or horse-drawn trains. The locomotives on the Stockton & Darlington Railway had not always been very reliable, and a couple of them blew up! But using stationary engines would have been very complicated – fifty-four stationary engines would have been needed to take trains from Liverpool to Manchester, and the chances were high of one or more of them breaking down and bringing the whole railway to a halt.

So the Liverpool & Manchester Railway Company decided to hold a competition to see whether they could find an improved locomotive. These were the Rainhill Trials of 1829. People were invited to enter their locomotives in a contest to see how powerful, reliable and cheap to run they were. The contest was held on a length of railway line at Rainhill near Liverpool, and thousands of people turned up to watch it.

Rocket, winner of the Rainhill trials and one of the most famous locomotives in the world. However, it too would be out of date within a year or two, as engine builders got to understand the design of locomotives better.

Novelty – *Rocket*'s main rival at the Rainhill trials. Stephenson said it had 'no guts' and his assistant John Dixon called it 'a new tea urn'.

Five locomotives were chosen as the finalists. One – *Cyclopede* – was horse-powered. Another, *Perseverance*, was old-fashioned and slow, and got damaged on the way to the trials. Neither of them passed the tests set by the railway company. *Sans Pareil* and *Novelty* were better, but suffered leaks and other breakdowns. The clear winner was George Stephenson and his famous engine, *Rocket*. This completed the trial without breakdown and pulled a 12.5-ton load at 12 miles an hour. On its own, *Rocket* could reach 29 miles an hour. The Rainhill Trials proved beyond doubt that locomotives were the best way of working a railway. The future of steam locomotion was decided and the railway opened on 15 September 1830.

The Great Western Railway

Merchants in the port of Bristol saw the railway between Liverpool and Manchester being built, and decided they would like one. This would link them to the main market for their goods, London. They looked around for someone to organise the design and building of the railway. At that time, there

From as early as 1840, locomotives like the Great Western's *Fire Fly* were capable of speeds of 50 miles an hour and more.

were almost no people with experience of doing that. Instead, they appointed a young man of twenty-seven. His reputation in Bristol came from winning a competition to design a bridge (which had not yet been built) and doing some improvements to Bristol's harbour. His name was Isambard Kingdom Brunel.

As usual, lots of people opposed the plan and the first application to Parliament – for just part of the route – was rejected in July 1834. The second application was approved in August 1835. Up to then, many of the railways that had been built had a gauge of 4 feet, 8.5 inches (about 144 centimetres). But Brunel had different ideas. He decided to build his railway to a broad gauge of 7 feet and 0.25 inches (about 214 centimetres). The reasons for this, and the trouble caused by the Gauge Wars – between the broad gauge and the standard gauge – are described in another part of the book.

Great Western broad-gauge locomotive *Iron Duke* hauling an express train at some time between 1847 and its withdrawal in 1871. These early locomotives could do nearly 80 miles an hour and used to average 59 miles an hour between London and Swindon. A replica of *Iron Duke* can be seen at the Didcot Railway Centre.

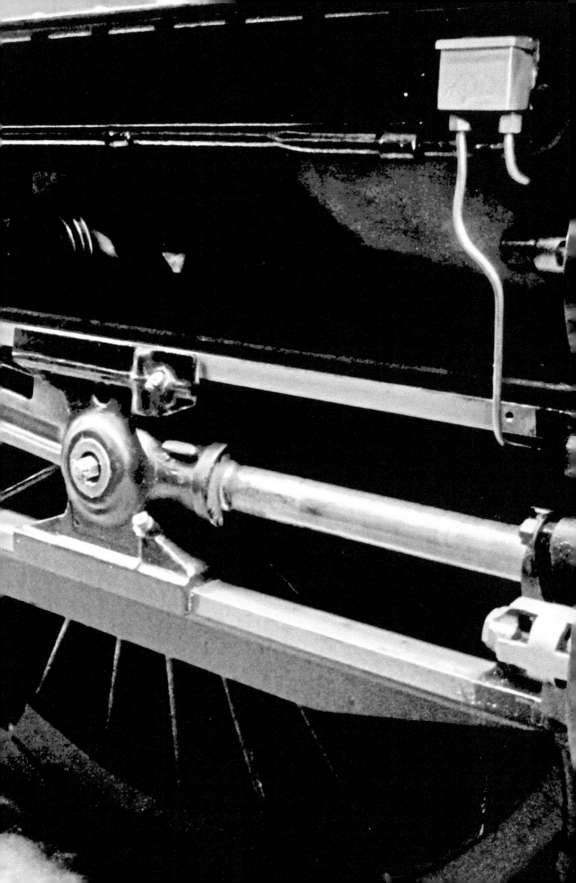

CHAPTER 2

THE VICTORIAN STEAM RAILWAYS

Here we look at a few of the main events affecting the railways during the nineteenth century.

The Gauge Wars

Many of the first railways were built miles away from each other, at different ends of the country. But people like George Stephenson soon saw that one day they would all be joined together. That could only happen if they were all built to the same gauge. So, as we saw, Stephenson made all his railways to a standard width of 4 feet, 8.5 inches (about 144 centimetres) between the rails. This was the width between the wheels of the farm carts near to where he lived. Many – but not all – of the early railway builders copied him.

As we also saw, Brunel and his broad-gauge Great Western Railway were the main ones who did not copy Stephenson. They built a railway with a 7-foot, 0.25-inch (about 214 centimetres) gauge. By 1845, many areas of southern and western England had broad-gauge railways. This soon started to cause problems, especially where the broad gauge met the standard gauge.

When that happened, the railways had to build a transfer shed. There, the broad-gauge train would stop at one platform and the standard-gauge train at the track on the other side of the platform. All the passengers, all their luggage and all the goods from the goods wagons then had to be moved from one train to the other. It took over a quarter of an hour to swap passengers

A transfer shed, with broad-gauge tracks on one side of the platform, standard-gauge on the other. Where the two gauges met, passengers, luggage and freight would all have to be moved from one train into the other.

and their luggage over, and it could take hours to swap over a freight train full of goods. This added greatly to the time and cost of travelling. People were very unhappy with this and, in 1845, the government set up a special group – a commission – to decide what to do about it.

It was clear that there had to be one gauge for all the main railways in Britain, but which one? Broad gauge was more expensive to build and run than standard gauge, but Brunel said that his Great Western trains were faster, more comfortable, safer and could carry more goods and passengers than the standard gauge. That was certainly true on the straight, flat railway he had built between London and Bristol. But it wasn't as good for railways in hilly areas, where the track would need to have a lot of bends.

There was another important argument against broad gauge. By 1845, most of the railways built in Britain had been standard gauge. At that time, there were only about 250 miles of broad gauge. It was fairly easy to convert broad gauge to standard gauge. You would not need to rebuild the broad-gauge tunnels, bridges, cuttings and embankments to take smaller standard-gauge trains. But converting railways the other way – from standard to broad gauge – would be very expensive indeed. You would almost have to start again with many parts of the standard-gauge railway to fit broad-gauge tracks on them.

The work of the commission led to a new law – the Gauge Act of 1846. This said that, in future, railways should normally be of Stephenson's standard gauge. They would, however, allow some narrow-gauge (less than 4 feet, 8.5 inch) lines to be built for local needs, and the Great Western could continue expanding its broad-gauge railway for the time being. This meant that, by 1860, the 250 miles of Great Western broad-gauge railway had grown to 544 miles.

From the 1870s the Great Western started making carriages that could be turned from broad gauge to standard gauge. They could saw them in half and make them thinner, mounting them on standard-gauge bogies. But not until 1877 did the Great Western stop building broad-gauge railway lines. From then on they concentrated on converting their tracks to standard gauge. The last 213 miles of broad-gauge railway were converted in a single weekend in May 1892. None of the original broad-gauge locomotives survive

No original locomotives survive today from the ending of the broad-gauge era in 1892. All we have are replicas, like those at the Didcot Railway Centre, and photographs. This Victorian picture is of *Xerxes*, a broad-gauge Great Western goods engine, in service between 1863 and 1882.

from those days, although modern copies of them can be seen at the Didcot Railway Centre.

Railway mania

In 1830 there were less than 100 miles of public railway in Britain (the rest were private). By 1850 the total had reached 6,000 miles. One of the reasons for all this growth was railway mania. Everyone saw that the first railways were very successful, and made a lot of money for the people who bought shares in them. Soon almost everybody wanted a share of those profits. In the 1830s and 1840s it seemed as if people had gone railway-share mad. Hundreds of proposals to build railways flooded in to Parliament. In 1845 alone there were 220 schemes for Parliament to consider. Some were sensible schemes, but a good number were not – the railway they wanted to build would never have enough customers to be profitable, or it copied a line that already existed, or the people promoting the scheme were simply swindlers. If all of the schemes that were proposed had been approved, there would not have been enough money in the country to pay for them, or enough people to build them.

All sorts of people, many who never normally invested in the stock market, rushed to buy railway shares. They often did not even need to have the money to pay for them. The way it worked was that you could become the owner of the shares by paying a small part of their price. The railway would then ask for the rest of the payment from you when they needed it, as the railway got built. The trick for the penniless shareholders was to sell their shares at a profit, before they were asked for the rest of the payment. This was all very well, so long as there was someone rich enough – or silly enough – to buy them.

But in October 1845 the market collapsed. Thousands of people were left with shares they could not sell, and many of them could not afford to pay the rest of the share price when the railway company demanded it. Many people were made bankrupt, or put into prison because of debts they could not pay.

In the end, the mad growth of the railways came to a stop. By 1850 the total length of new railway lines put to Parliament for approval that year came to just 6.75 miles. But the country would still be left with many miles

One of the National Collection of Railway Locomotives, *Shannon* was built in 1857 for the Sandy & Potton Railway. Over the years it worked as a shunter in the LNWR works at Crewe, on the Cromford & High Peak Railway and on the Wantage Tramway. *Shannon* was eventually bought by the Didcot Railway Centre, who got it working again long enough for it to take part in the Stockton & Darlington Railway's 150th anniversary in 1975.

of railway that would never be profitable, or which duplicated other lines. Many of these would become the railway closures of the twentieth century.

One of the biggest promoters of railways – known as the Railway King – was George Hudson. For a while he was one of the richest and most important men in the land and everybody wanted to be his friend. He founded the Midland Railway in 1844, and spent huge amounts of money buying up other railway companies and promoting new ones. However, he turned out to be one of the biggest swindlers of all. As his crimes were uncovered, he was forced to sell all his possessions and flee abroad to live in poverty for the next twenty years. Nevertheless, he did at least show the nation how Britain's railways needed to be organised, with a few large railway companies rather than the hundreds of little ones that had started off the railway age.

Different classes of travel

Long before the railways, there were different classes of travel. The very rich had their own private horses and carriages, with their own servants to drive them. Travellers on stagecoaches could either ride inside the coach, which was more comfortable, or outside on top, facing the heat and dust in summer and the rain and snow in winter. It all depended on how much they could pay for their fare. Those who could not afford stagecoaches at all might ride on a slow carrier's cart along bumpy roads, or simply walk.

In the chapter on passengers we look in more detail at the different classes of railway carriage in which people travelled. But the divide between the classes did not end there. Many larger stations had separate waiting rooms: they were either for first-class passengers (with comfortable chairs and a warm fire), second-class passengers (uncomfortable) or third-class passengers (very uncomfortable indeed). Then there could be different

Gladstone, the first in a class of thirty-six locomotives built for the London, Brighton & South Coast Railway from 1882. They were used to haul the heaviest expresses between London and Brighton. They started to be withdrawn before the First World War, but the last one remained in service until 1933. *Gladstone* is now part of the National Railway Museum collection.

classes of dining room and even ticket offices. Sometimes there were also separate waiting rooms for men and women.

However, the most comfortable travel of all was provided for the Royal Family. Queen Victoria made her first railway journey in 1842. She was a nervous passenger and the Royal Train was not allowed to go faster than 40 miles an hour. The preparations for a royal train journey were elaborate. Another train had to run along the same tracks in front of hers to make sure it was safe. No train (except a mail train) could pass on the opposite track and the whole length of the track had to be guarded against trespassers. A small army of special staff travelled with her, to fix anything that went wrong.

Wherever she was likely to visit regularly, the station got a Royal waiting room. At Slough, they even built a smart hotel opposite the station, mainly to be used as a waiting room for the Queen and any guests going to visit her in nearby Windsor Castle. Then Windsor got its

Luxury travel – the inside and outside of one of the royal carriages, made for Queen Victoria in around 1900.

own branch line, bypassing Slough, and the hotel went out of business. At Hatfield station, where the Queen sometimes went visiting, they built the platforms so that they were not opposite each other. This was so that, if a train was stopped at the opposite platform, its passengers could not stare at the Queen when she arrived. Nor were the royalty allowed to look at anything distressing, like a railway accident. On one occasion, there was a crash at Elderslie in Scotland, just before the Royal Train was due to pass. The railway company parked a whole train of empty coaches in front of the accident, so that the Royal passengers did not have to see it.

The navvies – the people who built the railways

Railway engines – especially the early ones – were not very good at going up steep hills. Nor were they very good at stopping when they were coming down steep hills! So railways needed to run on level ground, as far as possible. The trouble was that the world was not level. Railway builders had to deal with all sorts of hills and valleys along their routes. When they came to a hill, their choices were:

- to go round it, which made the railway longer and more expensive
- to build a tunnel through it
- to take a slice out of the hill – called a cutting – for the trains to run through.

If they came to a valley, they could either:

- build a bridge – called a viaduct – across it
- build an earth bank – an embankment – for the trains to run along.

Some of these works were huge. To take one example, the Sonning cutting near Reading is:

- 2 miles long
- at its highest point, about 20 metres deep (that is about 65 feet, or like four double-decker buses, piled on top of each other) and
- wide enough for four trains to go through at once.

The people who did these huge earth-moving jobs were called the **navvies.** The name is short for 'navigators', for they were the people who built the canals, also known as 'navigations', before the railways came along.

They did these works without bulldozers, excavators, lorries or any of the other machines we would use today. Mostly, all they had were pickaxes to loosen the soil, shovels to pick it up and wheelbarrows to carry it away. Sometimes they might have horses to help them pull the heavy wheelbarrows up steep slopes. If they came to solid rocks that were too big to be dug out, they might use gunpowder to blow them up.

They were very hardworking. A good navvy was expected to dig and remove sixty barrow-loads of earth each day. It was also very dangerous work – using pickaxes and shovels in slippery mud, pushing heavy wheelbarrows up steep and muddy hills, using explosives and digging tunnels. On some jobs, it was said that a navvy stood more chance of being killed or injured than a soldier did fighting in a battle.

All that hard work made the navvies very hungry and thirsty. They would eat two whole loaves of bread a day, two pounds of beef (about a kilogram, or enough for about eight grown-ups to have a meal), and would drink a gallon (five litres) of beer a day. In those days, everyone drank beer – even children – because water supplies were often full of germs. But the navvies' lives were very hard. Because they were always on the move as the railways got built, they had no permanent homes. Lucky ones might find a bed in a nearby house to sleep in as they travelled. Others might sleep in barns, sheds, or even in rough shelters made of tree branches in ditches. For all this work, they might be paid 25 pence a day. Not a lot, compared with what people earn today, but far more than they would have earned working on a Victorian farm – if there was even any work for them on the farm.

They were a strange mix of people. Some were farm workers who could no longer find work on the farms. Some were Irish, fleeing from the terrible famine in their own country. Some were criminals, on the run from the law. It was easier to hide among the navvies, partly because they often only knew each other by their nicknames. In one case, a navvy was asked the names of three of his fellow workers. All he could tell them was that their nicknames were the Duke of Wellington, Cat's Meat and Mary Anne, because of the hooked nose of one, what the second one used to sell and the high-pitched voice of the third.

The navvies were a wild and lawless bunch, and respectable people were terrified when they heard a new railway was heading towards them. Every payday, the navvies would drink far too much beer, start fights and get up to all sorts of other lawbreaking. They would sell their wives; if a pub ran out of beer, they had been known to knock it down; on a few occasions they even committed murders, and the police or even the army had to be called out to control them. But they were also badly treated by some of their employers, and were sometimes only reacting to that. Without the navvies, we could not have built all the railways that were made in Victorian times. Only towards the end of the nineteenth century, when most of the railways had already been built, did steam-powered machinery start to replace the muscles of the navvies.

Some of the navvies would become heroes. In the 1850s Britain was at war with Russia, and they were fighting in part of Russia called the Crimea. The British Army had big problems, because there were no proper roads there. They were not able to supply their fighting troops with the things an army needed. Nor could they carry the injured away from danger. One of Britain's biggest railway builders, Samuel Peto, sent a group of his navvies out to Crimea. They quickly built a railway from Balaclava to Sebastopol. This made a huge difference to the British Army. Suddenly the navvies, who were feared at home, became national heroes. Some people even thought they were going to fight the Russians with their pickaxes and shovels. Their work certainly helped the army to win the war.

Changing town and country – and people's lives

The Victorian railways made big changes to both the towns and countryside. In the towns and cities the railways took over huge areas of land. At their greatest, the railways themselves took over between 8 and 10 per cent of the land in the centres of our cities for their tracks, stations, goods yards and workshops. If you included land used by businesses related to the railways, the figure went up to about 20 per cent. The land where the poorest people lived was the cheapest so, whenever possible, the railway companies bought and built on that land. The poor people who lived there were just thrown out of their homes. Nobody built new houses for them, so they had to crowd into whatever cheap slum housing was left in the city.

Some historic towns and cities suffered badly at the hands of the railways. To give just three examples, Berwick's historic castle was almost destroyed by the building of the town's railway station, and what remained of Newcastle's ancient castle was left sitting in the middle of many lines of railway track. The ruins of the ancient priory at Lewes in Sussex had a railway line going right through the middle of them.

As we have seen, the railways needed a level track to travel on, so this also meant major changes to the countryside. People used to protest against many of these works, but gradually most people got used to them. Some even grew to like them! Railway buildings could also be the cause of disputes. Some were hated, but some were among the best buildings of Victorian times. For example, the big London railway stations are like great cathedrals of steam, and historic parts of the railway like the Forth Railway Bridge today have the highest level of protection we can give them.

Trojan started its life in 1897 working on the Newport & South Wales Docks Railway. This railway had 100 miles of dock sidings and a 10-mile passenger line, and became part of the Great Western in 1923. *Trojan* then worked in various parts of the Great Western until it was sold to a coal-mine railway in 1932. It is now at the Didcot Railway Centre.

Finally in this chapter, I have listed just a few of the ways railways changed people's lives in the nineteenth century:

- they made it possible for the first time to supply growing towns and cities with all the food, fuel and other goods they needed.
- they opened up the competition to supply food, fuel, etc. to a wider area and so made those things cheaper.
- they enabled people who owned businesses in towns and cities to live well away from their places of work. These were often the people who had been the leaders of their communities, and this could change the character of those towns and cities.
- they made it possible for people to visit places they would never have seen in the days before railways. For example, 6 million people visited the Great Exhibition in London over six months in 1851, and 5 million of them travelled there by rail.
- the railways not only changed the way wars were fought, but they also made it easier for governments to put down what they saw as troublemakers at home. Soldiers could quickly be sent to anywhere in the country, to deal with strikers and other protesters.
- they made national sports like football or horseracing possible.
- they helped make holidays and day trips to the seaside and other tourist attractions possible. The railways even created many seaside resorts.
- they also created towns that were built around the railways – Swindon and Crewe were just two examples.
- they changed the way we tell the time. Before the railways, everyone set the time according to when the sun rose over their town. But it rose at different times in different parts of the country. So the time at the most eastern and western parts of the country might be half an hour or more different. This made it very confusing to draw up railway timetables. So the railways got everyone to agree to the same time right across Britain. At first they called it railway time, but today we call it Greenwich Mean Time.

PICTURE GALLERY

NARROW GAUGE

Many railways were built to a narrower gauge than the standard 4 feet, 8.5 inches. They were cheaper to build and to run where big loads did not have to be carried, and were better at going round sharp corners.

Double-ended engines, like this one on the narrow-gauge Festiniog Railway, were a cunning way of dealing with the fact that steam engines are not always easy to drive backwards. This is a Double Fairlie, and was built in 1992 – the latest and most powerful addition to the railway. Others owned by the railway – some still operational – date from 1879.

Steam railways come in all sizes. Believe it or not, this Class 25 NC monster is a narrow-gauge locomotive! It was built in 1953 by the North British Locomotive Company. It was made for South African Railways to run on their 3-foot, 6-inch-gauge (1,067 mm) tracks, and can be seen at the Buckinghamshire Railway Centre.

Steam railways come in all sizes. This one is in Prospect Park, Reading.

Holiday crowds enjoy a 7-mile trip through the Lake District on the 15-inch gauge Ravenglass and Eskdale Railway.

The Talyllyn Railway and its locomotive *Sir Haydn*. This 2-foot, 3-inch-gauge railway opened in 1866 to carry slate from the quarry to the port of Tywyn. *Sir Haydn* dates from 1878 and was bought by the railway restorers for £25 in 1951. The Reverend Wilbert Awdry – author of *Thomas the Tank Engine* – was one of the volunteers who helped restore the railway, and his imaginary narrow-gauge railway at Skarloey in the books is modelled on the Talyllyn.

CHAPTER 3

RECORD BREAKERS! FASTEST AND FURTHEST

There are a number of records for steam engines to break. One is for the fastest speed over a short distance. Another is for the fastest speed over an entire journey. Often this is measured as a start-to-stop **average** speed (that is, from standing still at the platform at one end of the journey to standing still at the platform at the other end of the journey). Another type of record is for the longest non-stop journey – without having to stop to change locomotives, pick up new crew or fill up with coal or water. We will look at each in turn.

Fastest speed

Before the railways, the fastest any man had ever gone was on the back of a galloping horse. It was soon clear to some of the earliest railway builders that steam locomotives might go very much faster. But many people were frightened at the thought of these high speeds. Some – including a famous scientist of the day called Dionysius Lardner – said people would not be able to breathe going at such speeds and would die. This was nonsense, of course, but early railway builders like Stephenson and Brunel tried to keep quiet about how fast their engines might go, in case the people in Parliament took fright and refused to let them build their railways.

The first real test of steam locomotives – the Rainhill Trials in 1829 – set the competitors a low speed target. They had to pull a train at just 10 miles an hour. But during the trials Stephenson's *Rocket* did a demonstration run at almost 30 miles an hour. This was as fast as a galloping horse, except that *Rocket* could keep that speed up for much longer than any horse. A further, unhappy speed record was set on the opening day of the Liverpool & Manchester Railway in 1830. During the opening ceremony, a government minister named William Huskisson was run over and badly injured by a locomotive. The locomotive *Northumbrian* was used to carry him to hospital in Eccles. In their rush to get him there, the engine set a new record speed of 36 miles an hour.

A speed of 56.7 miles an hour was claimed on the Grand Junction Railway near Crewe in 1839 by a locomotive called *Lucifer*. By 1845 it was claimed that speeds of 60 to 65 miles an hour were fairly common on the Great Western broad gauge. But there were lots of problems with some of these early speed 'records'. Steam engines did not generally have speedometers until well into the twentieth century. The watches people used to time trains were not as accurate as modern ones and the people doing the timing were not so skilled at using them. Some of the measurements were taken over very short distances, like 100 yards. Readings taken over half a mile, with a stopwatch that could read tenths of a second, would have given a much more reliable result.

There were other things that could affect the results. Was the track on which the speed was recorded flat, or going uphill or downhill? How smooth and safe was the track? How heavy was the train the locomotive was pulling and how hard were the carriages to pull along? (Older carriages were generally harder to pull than newer, more efficient ones). But one trial that does seem to have given accurate results was carried out by the Great Western. Pulling a **dynamometer car** (a special carriage used for accurately recording a train's speed), this showed three of their locomotives – *Iron Duke*, *Great Britain* and *Courier* – each touching 78 miles an hour for a brief moment while going down Dauntsey Bank in Wiltshire in 1848. The Great Western would hold this record for the next forty years.

As for the standard-gauge railways, by the 1850s they also had engines that could run at 70 or even 75 miles an hour. However, other factors held them back from doing so. First, many of the tracks were dangerous. Their soft wrought-iron rails wore out quite quickly and the proper making of the track bed beneath the rails in order to give a smooth ride at speed – called the ballasting – was not yet properly understood. We now know that the track bed has to be shaped in particular ways, with the right type of stones laid on top, and it must be kept well drained and free of weeds. There were

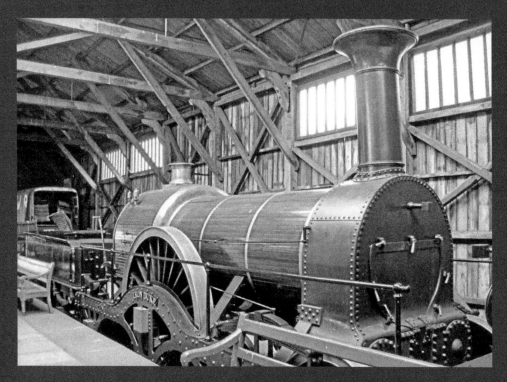

Iron Duke – a replica of the broad-gauge express locomotive that ran on the Great Western Railway between 1847 and 1871. This early locomotive held a world record of almost 80 miles an hour and used to haul the world's fastest passenger service, the *Flying Dutchman*. An Iron Duke Class locomotive worked the last broad-gauge passenger service in 1892.

other dangers. Until the 1870s, tender locomotives usually only had brakes on their tenders, not the locomotive itself, so they were not very good at stopping. Signalling was also still very primitive, and the interlocking of signals and points (explained in another chapter) to improve safety did not really start to be introduced until the 1860s.

There was also a lack of will by some railway companies. Going fast was expensive. It meant greater wear and tear on the locomotives and carriages. If your express trains were being filled with passengers while going at slower speeds, why bother going faster? For the London & North Western Railway, the timing of some of their express services was decided by their contract with the Post Office. This said they had to run the Irish Mail train between Euston and Holyhead at an average speed of just 42 miles an hour.

Long parts of the journey from London to Scotland during the Race to the North in the 1880s (which I will talk about shortly) were being done at an average of 60 miles an hour, or slightly more. For short spells some of the trains were doing more than 70 miles an hour and, in a couple of cases, it was claimed (but never proved) that trains reached 90 miles an hour. But at this time the fastest speed supported by real evidence seems to have been by a Great Western broad-gauge engine, *Lightning,* which recorded a speed of 81.8 miles an hour in 1887. This was not much faster than the maximum speeds that were being recorded forty years earlier. Some people thought steam engines could never go much faster.

However, improvements were being made, not just to the locomotives but also to the rails (made from new kinds of steel) and the track bed itself. All of these helped trains to go faster. Even so, it would still take until the 1890s for the speed record to be raised to 90 miles an hour.

The 1887 record aside, the Great Western had not been much involved in record breaking for some years, at least until its broad gauge was finally scrapped in 1892. But, towards the end of the nineteenth century, a Great Western engine once again took the record for the fastest properly measured speed for a locomotive. This one did 83.5 miles an hour on Wellington Bank, near Taunton. Nevertheless, by the very end of the century, two locomotives – one from the North Eastern Railway (No. 1517) and one from the Midland (No. 117) – were tied for fastest speed, with a maximum of 90 miles an hour.

The next major leap in record breaking was one that was kept secret for many years. In the days when ocean liners were the only way of travelling between Britain and America, the liners used to drop off their passengers at Plymouth. That meant they could get to London more quickly by train than they could by staying on the ship. There was an agreement that the London & South Western Railway would take the liner passengers bound for London, while the Great Western would take all the transatlantic mail. The journey to London for the two trains soon turned into a race. Once again, risks started to be taken, as difficult lengths of track were taken at high speed.

One of the locomotives hauling the Great Western Ocean Mail train was the *City of Truro*. On 9 May 1904, running down the Wellington bank (a scene of previous record breaking), the train was timed as covering a quarter of a mile in 8.8 seconds, which works out at 102.3 miles an hour. If this were accurate, she would be the first locomotive ever to go faster than 100 miles an hour. There was much controversy over the years about whether or not it did, and the arguments continue to this day, but some believe that the *City of Truro* did achieve at least 100 miles an hour. In fact, it could have been

City of Truro: In 1904, this Great Western locomotive was the first thought to reach 100 miles an hour (though the railway company did not want to own up to their record-breaking run!).

higher, had not the driver been forced to brake because of workmen on the track ahead.

But the Great Western did not officially admit to this achievement until 1922, despite an article in the following day's newspaper, hinting at a new record. The Great Western may have feared that their passengers would be frightened off by such extreme speeds. No aeroplane had ever gone that fast, and the world land speed record for motor cars only passed 100 miles an hour that same year. An experimental electric railway in Germany had claimed (if not proven) a speed of 130 miles an hour the previous year. The *City of Truro* is one record-breaking locomotive that has been preserved, and now lives most of the time at the Gloucestershire Warwickshire Railway.

By the early 1930s the German Nazi government was planning to make their railways the best in the world. As part of this, they wanted to have the fastest train in the world. They developed a streamlined diesel train called the *Flying Hamburger*, which they claimed had reached a speed of 124 miles an hour during testing in 1932.

Despite this, British railway designers did not want to move to diesel power. They thought they could still make steam engines go faster. Tests to look at using one of the German diesel trains on the East Coast route to Scotland also proved disappointing. The London & North Eastern Railway's famous locomotive designer, Nigel Gresley, had designed some powerful A1 Pacific locomotives and by 1934 these were starting to achieve maximum speeds of 100 miles an hour (unlike the *City of Truro*'s earlier effort, their speeds were public, and a generally accepted record). A train developed from the A1, which was an A3 called *Flying Scotsman*, became the first locomotive to have a properly timed speed of over 100 miles an hour, in 1934. Another A3, *Papyrus*, pushed the speed record up to 108 miles an hour in March 1935. But at these high speeds, Gresley saw the need for his locomotives to be streamlined. His next design, the A4, had sleek, streamlined bodywork that certainly looked as if it should go faster. Meanwhile the Germans were also developing new steam trains, leading to their new world speed record of 124.5 miles an hour in May 1936.

Back in Britain, from September 1935 the new A4s started running the Silver Jubilee service between London and Newcastle. They had not yet started to find out how fast the A4s could go, although they were achieving average speeds of 70 miles an hour and reaching a maximum of 90 miles an hour in places. Then, in August 1936, one of the A4s, pulling a normal train of passengers and not trying to make a record-breaking bid, reached 113 miles an hour – a new British record, although still slower than the Germans.

More A4s were delivered during 1937, this time painted in the blue of the Bugatti racing cars of that time, rather than the silver of the first few locomotives. But now new competition appeared, in the form of a streamlined locomotive called *Coronation* from the LNER's British rivals, the London Midland & Scottish Railway. It was designed by another famous locomotive engineer, William Stanier. This first ran on 29 June 1937 and set another new British record of 114 miles an hour on a stretch of line near Crewe.

This was a bad place for record breaking. They were still doing 110 miles an hour when they realised they were just a mile and a half from Crewe station, which has bends limited to 20 miles an hour. They slammed the brakes on, so hard that they caught fire, throwing the terrified passengers around and smashing the crockery in the dining car. But they were still doing 57 miles an hour – almost three times the proper speed – as they went through Crewe station. Somehow they managed to stay on the rails.

Some of the new batch of Gresley's A4s had improvements such as double chimneys fitted to them. These improved locos included one called *Mallard*, which came into service in March 1938. It was decided that *Mallard* would be the one to make the next attempt on the world record. The attempt was

No. 6220 *Coronation*, the first in a class of streamlined locomotives built for the London Midland & Scottish Railway in 1937. That same year she set a British speed record for a train, of 114 miles an hour. The streamlining was removed in 1946 to make her easier to repair, and she was scrapped in 1963.

to be made on 3 July 1938. It was a Sunday, so there were fewer other trains around to get in the way, and no paying passengers were allowed on the train.

Faster and faster through Lincolnshire went *Mallard* until, for just a quarter of a mile, the speed reached 126 miles an hour. A new world record had been set, beating the Germans by the narrowest of margins. *Mallard* was damaged in the attempt and limped into Peterborough for repairs, but she had won her place in railway history. Soon afterwards, the Second World War broke out and all thoughts of railway record breaking went from people's minds. Plans to try and get *Mallard* to do more than 130 miles an hour were dropped, and Nigel Gresley died during the war, in 1941. Right after the war, most nations' railways were in such a bad state that record breaking was impossible. Over the years that followed, many trains went faster than *Mallard*, but they were all diesel- or electric-powered. *Mallard* set a world record for steam locomotives that still stands and will probably never be beaten.

There is one final chapter to the steam railway speed record. *Bittern* is one of Nigel Gresley's A4 Pacifics, a sister to the record-breaking *Mallard*.

No. 464 *Bittern* A4 Pacific: *Bittern* is a twin sister to the record-breaking *Mallard*, one of Nigel Gresley's A4 Pacifics. Her work for British Railways ended in September 1966 and she was then owned by a series of enthusiasts.

She was built in 1937 and had a hard life during the Second World War, pulling extra-heavy passenger, freight and coal trains. As a sign of this hard work, Bittern has had fourteen boilers during her working life. Her work for British Railways ended in September 1966 and she was then owned by a series of enthusiasts.

Bittern is a record holder in her own right. In 2013, on the seventy-fifth anniversary of *Mallard*'s record run, *Bittern* was given permission to go faster than the normal British Railways limit of 75 miles an hour for steam trains on the main line. She reached a speed of 92.8 miles an hour, the fastest a preserved steam engine has ever achieved.

Fastest journey

Now we will look at the record for speeds across a journey overall. Despite all the problems with recording speeds in the early days, during the Gauge Wars of the 1840s it was decided that average journey speeds would be one of the ways the government would decide which of broad and standard gauge was better. They looked for two lengths of track – one broad gauge, one standard – that were of similar length and had similar running conditions. They chose London to Didcot for the broad-gauge tests, and Darlington to York for the standard gauge. Both tracks had almost no ups or downs. In the tests both locomotives turned in very similar performances, with an average speed of 46 or 47 miles an hour and top speeds of just over 60. However, in a later run, a newer broad-gauge train covered the line between London and Didcot at an **average** of 67 miles an hour.

By 1848 the Great Western could claim that the London–Didcot service was regularly doing a start-to-stop average speed of 66 miles an hour, from being stopped at the platform at Paddington to stopping at the platform at Didcot. This, or something very close to it, would remain a British railway and world record for the next fifty years or so. However, in the Gauge Wars, speed played only a very small part in deciding which gauge to choose. The main reasons for the choice of gauge are discussed in a previous chapter.

In some ways, the period between 1865 and 1888 was not one of the best for the railways of Britain. The trains did not get much faster and there were a number of accidents. Many of them were due to the railway companies failing to build the latest safety features into their railways. One railway manager even said that he would rather pay compensation to the families of the dead and injured in a railway accident than spend money on safety measures!

Things changed when rival companies started to race each other between London and Edinburgh in 1888. There were two main routes between the two capital cities – the East Coast and the West Coast. The East Coast took 9 hours and the West Coast 10. In November 1887 the East Coast companies announced that, for the first time, their *Flying Scotsman* service would include third-class passengers. They started attracting many customers away from the West Coast route. The West Coast companies decided to compete by providing a faster service. It led to a race that meant that, by August 1888, both sets of companies were doing the journey in just 8 hours. The West Coast companies even cut the passengers' lunchtime stop at Preston from 25 to 20 minutes to save time.

Changing engines at Grantham. The middle locomotive is one of Patrick Stirling's 'eight-footers', named for the size of its driving wheels. Fifty-three of them were built for the Great Northern Railway between 1870 and 1895, and they took part in the 1895 Race to the North. They could average 50 miles an hour pulling a 275-ton train, and had a claimed top speed of 85 miles an hour. When they were introduced, they were said to be the fastest locomotives in the world. They were gradually withdrawn between 1899 and 1916, but one of the class survives in the National Railway Museum.

Long parts of the journey were being done at an average of 60 miles an hour, or slightly more. For short spells some of the trains were doing more than 70 miles an hour and, in a couple of cases, it was claimed (but never proved) that trains reached 90 miles an hour.

A new 'Race to the North' started in July 1895, this time between the rival overnight services from London to Aberdeen. The West Coast companies suddenly announced that they were cutting 40 minutes off the timing of their service. One part of this competition was that the rival routes merged just to the north of Montrose and, after that, there was no way of overtaking. Whichever train got there first had first use of the tracks and the loser had to trail behind them for the final 38 miles of the journey. The North British Railway took this competition very seriously. They had some tricky track to travel along and their drivers started to take sharp bends and go through difficult junctions much quicker than the railway engineers said they should. This gave the passengers a ride that was often uncomfortable and sometimes terrifying!

Soon it turned into a real race. Speed limits and timetables were ignored and risks were taken as drivers looked for ways of cutting off every spare minute from the journey time. The western route was about 16 miles longer, but the eastern route needed an extra change of locomotive, which slowed them down. The western route finally won the race. On the night of 22/23 August, the 539 miles of the West Coast route were covered in just 512 minutes, an average speed of 62.3 miles an hour. In doing so, the train arrived in Aberdeen – at 4.32 a.m.

This shows why record breaking can sometimes be pointless. Why were the railway companies spending a lot more money to make their trains go faster, wearing their locomotives out more quickly and giving the passengers a very uncomfortable ride? All so that they could arrive in Aberdeen, hours before breakfast, while everyone else was still asleep!

Even so, these record-breaking speeds made rail passengers in other parts of the country jealous. Angry letters were sent to the newspapers, comparing the 'Race to the North' with the 'Crawl to the South'. Someone even sent in a comparison between a fish train on the North Western Railway with the luxury (first class only) passenger express between Brighton and London. The fish train was faster, proving (as someone put it)

The Cheltenham Spa Express, seen here just east of Reading, was in 1923 the fastest train service in Britain. At one stage, it had the world's first timetabled 70-mile-an-hour service, between Swindon and London.

that you were better off as a dead fish on the North Western Railway than as a live first-class passenger on the London, Brighton & South Coast line.

However, for start-to-stop journeys, the railways of 1900 still could not do much more than equal the average speed of 67 miles an hour, set by the Great Western broad-gauge locomotives way back in the 1840s.

The First World War put thoughts of record-breaking out of people's minds for ten years or so. However, in 1923 the Great Western's afternoon service from Cheltenham to Paddington was claimed to be the fastest scheduled train service in Britain and the world. It covered the 77.3-mile part of the journey between Swindon and Paddington (along Brunel's original Great Western line) at an average of 61.8 miles an hour. This was still slower than the 1840s Great Western record but, by 1929, they had cut 5 minutes off the journey time, increasing the average speed to 66.3 miles an hour. This world speed record only lasted for two years, for in 1931 two Canadian services beat it. The Great Western service was sped up again, first to 69.2 miles an hour, and then until it had a scheduled average speed of 71.4 miles an hour. It was the world's first regular service designed to run at an average of over 70 miles an hour, and became known as the Cheltenham Flyer, although its real name was the Cheltenham Spa Express.

This was not the end of the story. On 6 June 1932 the Great Western ran a special record-breaking service, in which they managed to do the Swindon–Paddington run at an average of 81.68 miles an hour. One unusual thing about the Cheltenham Flyer was that it was not only a record breaker, but also a very reliable service. It held the world record for overall journey speed until 1937, when one of the LMS's new *Coronation* Class took it from them, averaging 89.3 miles an hour over a journey of 69.9 miles from Welton to Willesden Junction.

Longest non-stop journeys

In the earliest days of steam railways, when the railway tracks were not linked up from one end of the country to the other, really long non-stop runs were not possible. Once the tracks were joined up by about 1850, three things limited how long a train could run without stopping – how much coal they could carry, how much water they held, and how long and how hard the crew could work.

The water problem was solved quite early on. In 1860 the London & North Western Railway became the first to fit long water troughs between their tracks. Locomotives could scoop up fresh supplies of water from them without stopping. The fireman would lower the scoop into the trough as they passed over the trough, and it would shovel the water up into a tank in the tender. The first one was installed on the route of the Irish Mail service, and meant that the service could run non-stop between Chester and Holyhead (84 miles). Soon most railway companies had troughs along their main lines, every 30 miles or so. Water no longer needed to limit the length of non-stop journeys. Even without water troughs, the Midland Railway in 1868 could manage a non-stop journey of 98 miles between London and Leicester.

The Victorian races to Scotland in the 1880s and 1890s were a good opportunity to try long-distance, non-stop trips. In the first Race to the North in 1888, the West Coast companies made what was then the world's longest non-stop run – 158 miles from London to Crewe. In the second Race to the North, in 1895, the London & North Western Railway went even further. They covered the 299.2 miles between London Euston and Carlisle non-stop, at an average speed of 51 miles an hour. However, these extreme long-distance runs were being done in the special case of the Race to the North. The longest regular non-stop daily run from 1896 was the 143.5-mile journey between Bath and Paddington on the Great Western. Racing conditions or not, the run from London to Carlisle would remain a British non-stop record until 1928.

No. 6100 *Royal Scot* – built in 1927 for the London Midland & Scottish Railway. She once held the record for the longest non-stop journey (which was then the 299 miles from Euston to Carlisle). The engine was displayed in the United States at the Century of Progress Exhibition in Chicago in 1933, and did a 'celebrity tour' of the USA and Canada. She was rebuilt in 1950 and withdrawn from service in 1962.

In that year the LMS made a non-stop trial run between London Euston and Glasgow, a distance of 401.4 miles. The tiredness of the crew was by now the biggest limit to non-stop travel. This London–Glasgow run was a severe test for the driver and fireman, who had to be on duty for the full eight-hour journey. In November 1936, the LMS did the same journey, but in two hours fewer. This time, they had an extra member of the crew on the footplate. He could take over as reserve fireman or engine driver, if needed.

Nigel Gresley had a different solution to the problem of the crew getting tired. From 1928 some of his locomotives had special tenders built, with tunnels through the middle of them. This meant that a fresh crew could get from the first carriage of the train onto the footplate and take over without the train having to stop. The tenders also carried 9 tons of coal. It meant that these locomotives could run the 392 miles from London to Edinburgh non-stop.

The current distance record for a non-stop journey by a steam engine rests with one of Gresley's A3 Pacifics, the famous *Flying Scotsman*. However, it was not set in this country. While visiting Australia in 1989, after her retirement from British Railways, the *Flying Scotsman* made a non-stop journey of 422 miles while travelling from Melbourne to Alice Springs.

No. 4472 *Flying Scotsman* is possibly the world's most famous locomotive. She was built in 1923 for the London & North Eastern Railway – another Nigel Gresley design – and spent 1924/25 as an exhibit in the British Empire Exhibition at Wembley. While in service in 1934 she became the first locomotive to be officially timed at 100 miles an hour. She used to pull non-stop services from London to Scotland. Withdrawn in 1963, she was then owned by a series of enthusiasts, who displayed her around the world. She is now part of the National Railway Museum collection.

CHAPTER 4

TWENTIETH-CENTURY RAILWAYS

The years before the First World War were, in some ways, some of the best for Britain's railways. The railway network was about twice as big as it is today. Steam engines were just about as good as they would ever get. The railways were getting more comfortable, better maintained and safer than ever before. They were also getting faster, as the chapter on speed records showed. Most of the railways were well run, and there was real pride among railwaymen in providing a smart, efficient service.

Competition

The railways had little competition from other modes of transport for most kinds of journeys. Lorries and cars were still slow, expensive and sometimes unreliable, and most of the roads were bad. The first aeroplane flight only took place in 1903 and, before the First World War, most people could not see a practical use for flying machines. More or less anything – or anyone – that needed to travel more than a very short distance went by rail.

However, there was starting to be some competition. Some suburban railways found themselves competing with the electric trams that started coming into urban areas from about 1900. The trams could run along the streets where people lived and could stop more often. So they were very convenient for passengers to use, and they were also cheap. There was also starting to be competition from tramways and the first petrol buses along some country routes where there were not many customers. On these, the railways could only afford to offer a few services a day. At the end of the branch line, the locomotive on a normal railway had to be turned around, run round to the back of the train and reconnected up to it. The trams were cheaper to run, and so could provide more services. They also could be driven from either end, so did not need to be turned around.

To deal with this competition, the railways came up with the Steam Rail Motor. This was a 'self-propelled single-carriage passenger train, which could be driven from either end'. It was cheaper to run than a normal train, could stop more often to pick up and drop off passengers and did not need turning round at the end of the line.

The Steam Rail Motors were very successful, but there were problems. They soon got overcrowded and the railway companies started adding extra carriages to them. This was a bad idea. They were not very powerful to begin with, and the extra weight slowed them down even more. Also, having the steam engine inside the carriage made it very difficult to keep the carriage clean. If work was needed on the motor, the whole train would be out of action.

These problems led the railways to develop the push-and-pull train. A normal locomotive was joined up to a specially adapted carriage. The locomotive either pushed or pulled the carriage, and the train could be driven from either end – the footplate or the carriage – without the need to turn it around at the end of the line. The Steam Rail Motor was important to the history of railways. It set the pattern for the types of modern train we have today on shorter-distance services – the diesel multiple units.

The other competition the railways had was with each other. Before the war, there were over 120 private railway companies. The governments had allowed many railways to be built that did the same thing as other lines, or that would never have many users. As a result, many of them were in wasteful competition with other railways. A number were losing money. As we will see in the chapter about the railways at war, the First World War changed a lot of things.

Wartime Railways

The railways made big changes to the way wars were fought. They made it much easier to move around large numbers of soldiers and all the equipment they needed, quickly and over long distances. They also made it easier for large armies to stay in one place, since they could now have all the food and equipment they needed delivered to them. A famous German General named Ludendorff once said it was more important to have railway lines than guns.

From their earliest days, governments recognised how important railways would be in wartime. Laws were passed from 1842 onwards to make sure troops and their equipment could be moved when and where the government wanted, and for a standard price. By 1855, Britain was fighting a war against Russia in a part of Russia called the Crimea. As we saw, the British troops were bogged down until a group of navvies went to Crimea and, in just seven weeks, built an eight-mile railway between the port and the front line. The Grand Crimean Central Railway (as they called it) transformed the war. But I want to concentrate on what it was like back in Britain, using the railways during the war years.

From 1871 government control of the railways in Britain went further. They now had the power to take over the running of the railways completely if there were a war. This first happened in the First World War, in 1914. A controlling government body had already been set up in 1912, expecting war. They decided which journeys would be most important. Top of the list came all the needs of the war effort – moving troops and their equipment, and the things needed to make their weapons and power their ships and lorries. Then came the trains delivering the food, coal and other essentials that the people at home needed. Passengers, travelling for business or pleasure, were at the bottom of the list. This meant that passenger services often got delayed or cancelled, or were held up as military trains went first. To add to their troubles, the ordinary passenger saw their fares increased by half from January 1917 and the cost of freight transport also went up.

It became very difficult for the railways to operate. 675 of their engines, 30,000 wagons – even some 2,300 miles of their rails – were sent over to France and to other places, to be used where the war was being fought. Over 30 per cent of the nation's railway workers volunteered to join the army and navy, despite the railway companies trying to stop them. It got so bad that some of the railway workers had to be taken out of the army later, to be brought back home and keep Britain's own railways running.

So the railways had less equipment and fewer workers, but the government still demanded a lot of extra services to be run. In just the first two weeks of the war, they arranged 1,408 special trains to carry 334,500 troops and their guns, horses, vehicles and stores. All of this work meant that the trains did not get properly maintained, and were wearing out more quickly.

The peacetime railways were not designed for war conditions. For example, the railways in the north of Scotland were single-tracked, quiet lines in peacetime. Suddenly they had to carry huge amounts of coal, supplies, equipment and sailors to the Royal Navy's main bases, such as Scapa Flow and Cromarty Firth. No other railway went there, and the nation's security depended on the navy getting its supplies. The Highland Railway could not cope and nearly broke down completely. Within a year of the war starting, two thirds of their locomotives were either completely broken down or in urgent need of repair. The other railway companies had to help them out by lending locomotives and wagons.

Many more dangerous loads had to be carried by the wartime railways in both wars. On one occasion, eighteen wagons of poison gas shells broke loose from their train and started rolling away. Only quick action by a signalman stopped them crashing and causing an environmental disaster. Come the end of the war there was a huge argument about how much the government should pay the railway companies for wearing out their railways. The government refused to pay anything near what the railways thought they were owed. Companies like the Highland Railway had no hope of paying for all the repairs their worn-out railway needed.

One cost of the war to the railways that no one had counted on was the army selling off all the lorries they no longer needed. These were bought by people who used them to compete for customers with the railways. They either carried goods or had seats fitted and were converted into buses. All in all, the First World War did a lot of harm to the railways.

All of these problems were repeated when the Second World War began. But another terror was added – war from the air. The enemy bombers now had the power to do major damage to towns, cities – and railways. The railways became an important target for German bombers.

Like all our towns and cities, the railways introduced a blackout. Locomotives had canvas covers over their cabs to stop the glow of their fires being seen by bombers, though it also made it very hard for the drivers to see where they were going. Carriages had their windows painted black, and only the dimmest of lights shining inside. Stations too were blacked out and even the station's name was painted out, to stop any invaders knowing where they were. Confused travellers would get out at the wrong station (or fall out of the train, if it stopped between stations). They would trip over unseen obstacles and fall off the edge of the darkened platform. Not least, it became very difficult for all the railway workers to run the railway – working in darkness, affected by bombing, suffering shortages of workers and supplies and trying to patch together trains that needed repair.

Trains for the general public would once again be held up or cancelled, giving way to military traffic. People's journeys would be slow, uncertain, overcrowded and uncomfortable. They could spend hours waiting at a signal, to travel behind a military train that was being allowed to go first. There would be no food for the journey, no paper or soap in the toilets.

Huge numbers of people and materials had to be moved. In the first weekend of the war about 1,500,000 children and others had to be evacuated from the main cities, for fear of bomber attacks. In about a week in the spring of 1940, 620 special trains carried about a third of a million exhausted soldiers away from the south coast, as the British army was evacuated from Dunkirk. In the second half of 1944, 14,763 special freight trains carried the supplies the forces landed in France needed. In just six days after D-Day, 271 special trains carried almost 100,000 troops to the port of Southampton. In the war as a whole, 538,559 special trains carried either troops or their supplies. This was done despite the government taking over 340 of the companies' locomotives for use in the war overseas.

Posters would ask the traveller 'Is your journey really necessary?' It certainly was not enjoyable. But many people decided their journey was necessary. Passenger and freight travel increased hugely. By 1942 passenger travel had increased by 50 per cent over pre-war levels, because the alternative of going by car was ruled out by petrol rationing. As for freight, the amount of traffic was up by about 40 per cent. Not only was road freight transport difficult, coastal shipping could not carry goods, for fear of submarine attacks. All of those deliveries had to be moved onto the railways.

Then there was the bombing. Huge damage was done to parts of the railways, though the repairs teams got really good at fixing it in a very short time. In all, the railways suffered 10,000 air-raids, losing them 14,000 carriages and 24,000 goods wagons, not to mention the loss of life. Even if the bombs did not hit the railway, an unexploded bomb within 400 yards of a railway line could bring services to a halt, for fear that the shaking from the railway could set it off.

The railway locomotives were asked to pull more and more, and heavier and heavier trains, but were getting less and less maintenance. An engine could go 100,000 miles between major overhauls. All the railway works that should have been fixing trains were busy making parts for submarines, tanks and other war materials. Once again, many of the skilled railwaymen who would have done the maintenance were in the armed forces or civil defence – about 110,000 of them by the end of the war.

The railways were in a shocking state by the end of the Second World War. Most of the damage to them had been done by the British government, rather than by German bombers. Air raid damage would cost £30 millions (at 1946 prices) to repair. But lack of maintenance of the railways during the war years would cost £151 millions to put right. Then there was the investment in new railway equipment that was now needed, after almost nothing had been spent on it through all the war years.

The government owed the railway companies a huge debt for wearing their railways out – much more than they could afford to pay. The railway companies could not afford to put things right, and no private person would put their money into such a worn-out railway. So instead the government took the railways into public ownership, as we see in another chapter.

After the First World War: Grouping and the Big Four

One lesson that everyone learned from the First World War was that the railways worked better under a single management; but the government did not want them to stay under their control. Instead, from the start of 1923, they put most of the nation's railways into one of four groups of private companies – the Big Four, or the Grouping, as it was called. The Grouping consisted of the Great Western Railway (GWR); the London and North Eastern Railway (LNER); the London Midland and Scottish Railway (LMS); and the Southern Railway (SR).

There was not much choice about grouping the railways. Some of the small railway companies had been so hard hit by the war that they probably could not survive on their own. The Big Four brought together the biggest and smallest of railways. In the case of the Great Western, it united the Great Western Railway itself, which had 3,005 miles of track, with many dozens of much smaller companies, such as the Forest of Dean Central Railway, which only had 5 miles. This was not such a big change as it may seem. The Great Western had taken over many smaller railways over the previous eighty years, going back to 1843. Also, a number of the railways they took over in 1923 were already operated by them or leased to them. In fact, the Great Western was much less changed than some of the others. Both the LMS and the LNER had to deal with railways that stretched from London to the north of Scotland. Many people in Scotland and the north did not like their railways being run from London, instead of being local. Also, the combining of so many little railways meant the new companies had a mass of different locomotives and wagons. For example, the LMS found itself with 10,316 locomotives in 1923 – but they were of 393 different kinds. This made it very difficult to keep them all in good working order.

Some of the main developments of the period from 1923 to 1948 were:

- That the railways had to invest heavily after the war years to replace worn-out locomotives, wagons, carriages and tracks. This was difficult, because the government never paid them properly for all the wear and tear on the railways during the war;

- that speed became glamorous, and companies competed with each other to be seen as the fastest, most modern and most comfortable;
- that competition from road transport was growing. As the Second World War approached, the railways campaigned to be given fair treatment in competing with the lorry and the bus. Some changes in 1933 gave the railways greater freedom and put more controls and more taxes on lorry traffic. But there was never really equal treatment and the big four railway companies never made a healthy profit in this period;
- that little-used branch lines began to be closed, especially from the end of the 1920s.

Looking at each of the Big Four railways in turn:

- The **London, Midland & Scottish** was the biggest transport business in the world. In 1938 it had more than 7,100 route miles (route miles are the distance between two points along the length of the railway, and never mind how many tracks there are linking those two points – so two towns ten miles apart count as ten route miles, whether there are one or four lines linking them). But the LMS did not make a lot of money, and it brought together two companies (the Midland and the North Western) who had been fierce rivals before grouping. They continued fighting after the merger. Their main routes were the West Coast Main Line to Scotland and the Midland Main Line, linking London to the industrial Midlands and North-West. This railway was more to do with freight traffic than passengers;
- The **London & North Eastern Railway** served the areas to the east and the north of London, right up as far as Aberdeen and Inverness. It had 6,590 route miles of track and its main works were in Doncaster. Two-thirds of its money came from freight, including moving one-third of Britain's coal. But it liked to present itself as a glamorous, fast passenger service, and their locomotive *Mallard* took the world speed record for a steam train;
- The **Great Western Railway** had 3,800 miles of track after the grouping. One of its major customers – the Welsh coal industry – was in decline as ships switched to diesel. By the 1930s the railway itself was the biggest customer for Welsh coal. Unlike some of the other companies, the GWR did not go in for streamlined express engines, but they did develop successful streamlined diesel railcars from 1933 onwards. Many of these remained in service until the 1960s;
- The **Southern Railway** covered the smallest area of Britain, in the south and south-east of England. However, it carried more than a quarter of

the country's passenger traffic on its 2,186 route miles of track. Its main activity between the wars was electrifying most of its railways, using the third rail system. Not all of the Southern Railway was electrified, so they did keep some steam locomotives. The Southern would be the worst affected of the Big Four during the Second World War. Before the war, only 25 per cent of its traffic was freight. But this increased by four or five times during the war years, while the number of passengers stayed about the same. The Southern was also the hardest hit by German bombing, being nearest to the enemy and having London at its heart.

After the Second World War: Nationalisation

When peace was declared, the railways were once again in very poor condition. They had been under government control again, and they had been made to do a lot more work during the war. They had to pull a bigger number of heavier trains, and got no new investment and very little maintenance. They had also suffered serious losses from German bombing – 482 locomotives, 13,314 carriages and 16,132 wagons had been damaged, while stations, tracks and other parts of the railway had also been bombed. There was more new competition after the war, not just from more lorries left over from the war, but also from war surplus aeroplanes.

But the war damage was not as serious as that in France, Germany and other parts of Europe. In those countries, they had no choice but to rebuild their railways completely. So they ended up with brand-new railways. In Britain, we ended up with patched-up old ones. There was a huge shortage of investment in the railways. The government itself worked out that between 1938 and 1953 the shortage of investment came to £440 million (or £11 billion at 2005 prices). It was clear that the railway companies could not make up the shortfall. The railways would have to be taken over by the government (nationalised).

The Transport Act 1947 came into effect at the start of 1948. It took almost all forms of mass transport under government control. The Big Four railways were now organised into six regions. The Southern and Western areas did not change. All the Scottish railways formed a single new region. The London Midland region kept all the old LMS lines in England and Wales, and the LNER was split into the Eastern and North Eastern regions, dividing the old LNER in England between north and south of Doncaster (these last two were eventually joined back together again). The first priorities of the railways were:

- to repair bomb damage;
- to do all the maintenance that had not been done during the war; and
- to replace all the locomotives, carriages and wagons that had been lost during the war.

The railways were now under the control of a new body, the British Transport Commission. They were in charge not just of railways but also of other transport, like canals, docks and harbours. This meant that some of the railways' money went to those other forms of transport.

At first, the regions operated like the old Big Four companies had done. There was no central control. They were all building different designs of locomotives and wagons. Some of the designs came from before the wars. The oldest dated back to 1898! British Railways was being left with equipment that was out-of-date, unreliable and a mess of different types that were difficult to maintain.

Only in 1951 did the British Transport Commission start to do something about it. They agreed a series of standard steam locomotives and carriages for all the regions to build, using the best features from all the pre-nationalisation companies. These designs were supposed to be long-lasting, but most of these locomotives would be withdrawn by the 1960s.

By December 1954 the railways were ready to think beyond repairing war damage. They published their Modernisation Plan. The government said modernisation would stop the railways making a loss by 1962. It would increase speed, safety, reliability and capacity, and win back a lot of the customers rail had lost over the years. The plan would cost a huge amount of money, but the government was not going to pay for it. The railways would have to pay for it all, and it was far more than they could ever afford.

The plan was unrealistic in all sorts of other ways. It tried to take the railways back to how they had been in their glory days, rather than looking at the changes that had happened to the way people and goods now travelled. The main thing about it, for steam train fans, was that it spelt the end for steam railways – at least as part of the national rail network. Diesel and electric trains would replace them. How was that decision made?

CHAPTER 5

THE END OF STEAM

Most people today love steam railways. It may make you wonder why we ever changed to diesel and electric trains. In fact, we were very late in making the change. Other countries went over to the new types of engine long before us. Most of our railways were steam-hauled until the Second World War, but there were experiments with other kinds of power. A Mr Volks built his first electric railway along Brighton seafront in 1883 and the London Underground started running electric trains in 1890. (Smoky steam trains running in underground tunnels were never popular.) Between the First and Second World Wars, the Southern Railway built a good many electric railway lines.

The real problem arose in 1948, after the government took over ownership of the railways. As we saw, the steam locomotives they had were nearly all worn out – they had had to work very hard during the war and had not been looked after properly. But with what were British Railways to replace them? The choices came down to new steam engines, diesels or electric trains. They started thinking about the case for and against each. While they were thinking about it, they were still ordering more new steam engines – orders were being placed right up until 1951. These engines could have a working life of forty to fifty years, so it could have been the twenty-first century before the last ones wore out. So what were the good and bad things about each of the choices?

The case for steam

Steam locomotives were a tried and tested type of railway engine, and they were quite cheap to build. British Railways already had a lot of them (in 1955

No. 34027 West Country class *Taw Valley*: Many of the Southern Region West Country and Battle of Britain classes of engine had their air-smoothed bodywork removed in the 1950s. *Taw Valley* lost hers in 1957. This is what they looked like without it. *Taw Valley* can be seen on the Severn Valley Railway at Bridgnorth.

they had 17,995 steam engines, compared with just 456 diesels, and most of them shunters). There were also companies already skilled at making steam engines, but not diesels. The coal needed to run them was cheap and Britain had a lot of it – so the government would not have to pay other countries to supply fuel (this was important, because the British government had no money after the war). Also the British miners, who were a powerful group, would have been very angry if the country had stopped using coal to power its railway engines. Some of them might have lost their jobs. We had lots of people already trained to drive and look after steam engines. It would not require any changes to the railways themselves to continue running steam engines on them, and the latest steam engines were almost as efficient as the early diesel locomotives. But there were also a lot of arguments against steam.

The case against steam

Steam engines were noisy, dirty and smelly. It took a lot of work to run and maintain steam engines – you could not use them 24 hours a day.

Supplies of the best British steam coal were running out, and using poorer coal meant steam trains did not run so well. (They even tried some experiments running steam engines on oil, instead of coal. This might have been a good idea, if the government could have afforded the fuel. It would have reduced maintenance costs, made them able to work for more of the day and increased their capacity for hauling trains.) Steam engines did not work well going backwards, so branch lines ideally needed turntables, and time was wasted turning the engines around and attaching them to the other end of the train at the end of the line (although the Steam Rail Motor idea – described elsewhere in the book – got around this problem). The poor visibility from a steam engine could even be a problem going forwards.

A lot of the work involved in looking after steam engines was hard and dirty; in the 1950s many people no longer wanted to do those kinds of jobs when there were plenty of easier, cleaner jobs to go to. The railways were having to compete with road and air transport for customers, and steam engines looked old-fashioned beside the latest buses, lorries and aeroplanes. Some of the steam engines from the days of Queen Victoria were still being used after the Second World War.

The case for diesel trains

Diesels could be started instantly and could be used 24 hours a day. It was said that one diesel engine could do the work of two steam engines. To illustrate this, *Mallard* covered 1,426,261 miles in its twenty-eight years of mainline running; the diesels that replaced it each did 2 million miles within fifteen years. Diesel trains could have a cab at each end of the train, and so did not need to be turned around at the end of the journey. They were easier to maintain and drive, and usually had shorter journey times than steam trains.

The case against diesels

Like steam engines, diesels were also rather noisy, dirty and smelly. Their technology was not yet proven (and some of the early ones were very unreliable, although diesel shunting engines had been a success). The

Shunting engines were the only proven success of diesel over steam when the great Modernisation Plan of 1955 was being put into effect.

railway workforce would need to be taught how to operate and maintain them. They tended to be rather heavier than steam engines, which meant more wear and breaking of the tracks. Importantly, their diesel fuel had to be imported from other countries and the government had no money to pay for it. Diesel engines could not heat carriages that used steam heating. They would need a separate boiler to do that. Lastly, in very cold weather – minus 9 degrees centigrade – diesel fuel froze (though it rarely got that cold in Britain).

The case for electric trains

They were the really clean, quiet and non-smelly option (the smelly bit – generating electricity, which could involve burning coal – was often done well away from the railway). This was important, because there was a big campaign in the 1950s to reduce air pollution. Electric locomotives were simpler to make and maintain and they were not as heavy as steam locomotives, and so put less strain on the tracks. Unlike diesels, the technology had been tried and tested in parts of Britain and overseas. Unlike with most steam engines, you could drive an electric train from either end. Last and possibly least, an electric train did not produce a lot of smoke in tunnels.

The case against electric

The really big argument against electric trains was the huge cost of converting the railways to electric power. Not only did you need new electric trains, you needed electric power lines along all of the tracks they would use. Unlike steam or diesel trains that carried their fuel with them, electric trains could not run along lines that had not been electrified. They also had to have new power stations to produce all the electric power the engines needed. Another problem was that many people thought the overhead power lines were an ugly addition to the countryside. There were already different electrical systems (based on third rail or overhead cables) and these did not work with each other. Would they all need to be converted to a single, standard system, and was that even possible? The third rail system was dangerous to trespassers and workers on the railway, and could not be used at all in railway depots, in case workers stepped on it. The third rail also tended to ice up in cold weather.

The end of steam

British Railways published their Modernisation Plan in 1955. Diesel and electric engines were to be the future of the railways. Steam would be phased out within fourteen years (by 1969). The trouble was, as we saw, that a lot of new steam engines had already been ordered. It would be five years (1960) before the last of them was delivered. So under the Modernisation Plan they would have a working life of less than ten years, although, as we saw, they could really last for forty or fifty years. Even so, by the end of 1960, the railways' stock of steam engines was down to 13,271, and in another eight years they were all gone.

No. 45379 LMS Black Five: The Black Fives were one of the most common sights pulling British Railways trains after the war. A 4-6-0 mixed-traffic tender locomotive, it was designed by William Stanier and 842 of them were built between 1934 and 1951. Why 'Black Five'? '5' was its power rating and 'black' was the colour they were always painted. This one was built in 1937. There are eleven Black Fives on preserved railways, including this one at the Mid-Hants Railway. The Black Five was so good, when British Railways came to design their standard locomotive types after the war, they copied the Black Five with almost no changes. Black Fives were still in use on the last day of main-line steam, although this example was retired in 1965. Enthusiasts bought it for restoration in 1974.

In their rush to replace steam with diesel quickly, British Railways made a lot of mistakes. Instead of having just a few standard types of locomotive, they ordered a lot of different types of diesel locomotives, before some of them had been properly tested. Some of them came from companies who were not used to making diesel locomotives. Sometimes these new diesels had to be scrapped before the steam engines they were supposed to replace.

As part of their Modernisation Plan, British Railways had decided to scrap 16,000 steam locomotives and 650,000 wagons. Scrapyards around the country bought up the wagons and any spare rails, broke them up and sold the scrap metal. The locomotives were more difficult to break up. At first the railway companies said that only they themselves would be allowed to break up the locomotives, but they soon found that there was too much work involved. They asked some private scrapyards to do it for them. One of these was at Barry, South Wales. They bought 297 locomotives from British Railways, along with a lot of old wagons and other scrap metal.

The people at Barry scrapyard soon decided that it was easiest to scrap the wagons first, leaving the more difficult locomotives until later. So the engines just stood out in the rain, rusting. By August 1968, 217 locomotives were still at the scrapyard. All the people who wanted to save steam locomotives for the future started coming to the yard, asking to buy them. At first, the engines were complete, or nearly complete, and could be towed to their new homes by a diesel locomotive. As they got more rusty and harder to move, they had to be taken out by road. Some enthusiasts could not afford to pay the full price of a locomotive at once. The scrapyard let them pay a deposit, and saved their engine for them until they had the rest of the money.

Sometimes engines had parts missing, and people were allowed to take spare parts off other engines to make theirs complete. There was also some stealing by souvenir hunters. 213 locomotives were saved from the Barry scrapyard, and over 100 of them have been restored so far.

Who were the preservers?

The Great Western Society is just one of about 100 railway preservation groups around the country. When the Great Western broad-gauge railway was finally scrapped back in 1892, none of the engines were saved for the future. When steam was scrapped entirely in the 1960s, the railways did a little better. In April 1961, *Railway Modeller* magazine announced that seventy-one different British Railways steam locomotives were to be preserved after main-line steam disappeared. But only ten of these were to be Great Western engines. They did not include some of people's favourite examples, like the Hall or Manor Class locomotives. A group of schoolboy Great Western enthusiasts decided to do something about it.

They launched an appeal in the August 1961 *Railway* magazine to raise enough money (£1,130) to buy an 0-4-2 tank locomotive. They managed to raise the money to buy it by April 1964. By 1967 they were known as the Great Western Society. They owned three locomotives and a number of carriages, and had use of the locomotive shed at Didcot, which British Railways no longer needed. Today they are a charity, with a stock of railway

An abandoned locomotive awaits restoration – or scrapping.

material worth more than £12 million. As for that first engine, No. 1466, it ran at the Didcot Railway Centre until 2000. It is now in the queue for another restoration, which may cost £150,000.

Doctor Beeching and railway closures

At about the same time as steam was disappearing from our main-line railways, many of the railway lines themselves were being closed. As we have seen, in the nineteenth century the railways grew in a very wasteful way. Lines were allowed to duplicate each other, or to go to places where there would never be enough business to make the railway worthwhile. Added to that, from the end of the First World War, the railways began to face real competition from road transport. The railways had to meet the heavy cost of keeping all their track in good order. Road traffic did not have the same problem. Much of the cost of repairing their 'tracks' (the roads) was met by the government. From the 1920s, unprofitable passenger railway lines started to be closed, with about 1,300 miles of them gone between 1923 and 1939.

After the Second World War the railways came under government control and the closures continued. Another 3,000 miles had gone by 1960. A protest group, the Railway Development Association, was set up to oppose the closures. But they were up against powerful groups of roads supporters, who wanted even greater cuts in the railways. One group, the Railway Conversion League, wanted to turn every railway in the country into a road.

The railways were losing huge amounts of money, and those losses were growing. In 1960 the government brought in a businessman from outside the rail industry to see what could be done. His name was Doctor Richard Beeching, and his job was to make the railways pay for themselves. To many railway lovers, Doctor Beeching was just a wicked man who closed down railways without thinking about how it would affect people's lives – but the truth is not as simple as that.

Beeching's first report came out in 1963. It found that one third of the total mileage of tracks was carrying just 1 per cent of the passengers, and half of all the stations combined took less than 2 per cent of the railways' ticket money. Beeching said that 6,000 miles of track should be closed entirely, along with 2,363 stations. By the 1970s the national rail network looked like the network of the 1850s. Some of the track that remained would be for freight only. But freight would also be affected – Beeching said a third of a million freight wagons should be scrapped.

People complained about the effect these closures would have on their communities. Beeching understood this – and said so in his report – but it was not part of the job he had been given to consider it. It was the job of the government to decide if the harm to communities was more important than saving money. In many cases the government decided that it was not. They even changed the rules about closing railways (in the Transport Act 1962) to make it easier to close them without thinking too much about the effects on the community.

Beeching produced a second report in 1965. This was much more extreme. It would have meant most of Wales, Scotland and East Anglia having no railways at all. But by then there was a new government, one that supported railways more. They rejected his report and Doctor Beeching soon left the railways and returned to business.

One good thing for steam railway fans came out of Beeching's work. Steam engines were already disappearing from Britain's railways before he came along, and steam lovers were starting to think about how they might be preserved. Many of the lines Beeching closed ran through attractive pieces of countryside. They were ideal for setting up heritage railways, and opposition to the Beeching closures may have got more people interested in the steam railway idea. Quite a few of Beeching's closed lines became heritage railways. Partly as a result of this, the British Isles now have almost as many heritage railways as the rest of Europe combined.

DID YOU KNOW ...?

- That the horses that pulled the earliest railway wagons sometimes got a free ride, in something called a dandy cart. When they came to a downhill section of railway, the horse was uncoupled from the wagon and was trained to jump onto the dandy cart at the back of the train. There, he could eat hay while the train rolled down the hill. It meant the horse got more rest and so could do more work going uphill.
- That before the first steam railways, the Oystermouth Railway tried powering their train with sails.
- That Richard Trevithick's 1804 steam locomotive was so slow that the driver did not ride on it, but walked beside it. His later locomotive, *Catch Me Who Can*, went rather faster, and its nickname was *Captain Trevithick's Dragon*.
- That the first railways had policemen before most towns and cities had police to patrol the streets. The very first proper police force – the Metropolitan Police – was only set up in 1829.
- That an early nickname for the policemen who patrol our streets was 'bobby'. Since the first railway policeman also acted as human signals to the engine drivers, modern railway signalmen still have the nickname of 'bobby' today.
- That in the early days of steam railways it cost eight times as much to build a mile of railway in Britain as it did in the United States, and three to four times as much as it did in Germany. Over a third of this was due to the cost of getting Parliament to agree to it. In some cases, it cost the railway more to get permission to build the railway

than it cost actually to build it. Most of the rest was due to the higher standards to which we built our railways. In the earliest days, too, a lot was spent on making the lines very flat, because the early engines could not cope with slopes. The engines built a few years later could manage them much more easily.

- That when Magnus Volk introduced the first electric railway along the seafront at Brighton in 1883 people were terrified of the electric third rail. To prove it was safe, the engineer removed his trousers and sat on the rail! Don't try it! If you sat on a modern electric third rail, you would not live for long!

- That the containers you see on modern goods trains are not a new idea. Isambard Kingdom Brunel thought of something very similar in the 1840s to make it easier to transfer goods between his broad-gauge and standard-gauge trains.

- Why the navvies, who built the first railways, tied strings round the legs of their trousers? It was because, when they were digging in the ground, they used to disturb the nests of all sorts of creatures, including rats and snakes. These creatures would rush out of their

The Forth railway bridge.

nests, looking for somewhere warm and dark to hide. Where better to hide than up your trouser leg? The strings kept these creatures out.

- That the world's greatest railway bridge, the Forth Bridge, was opened in 1890. It is made of 54,000 tons of steel and is held together by 6,500,000 rivets (the rivets alone weigh 4,000 tons). Fifty-seven men died building it and it used to take twenty-nine men about three years to paint it, using 45,000 litres of paint. As soon as they finished painting at one end, they had to start again at the other.

- That a man named William Brunton invented a walking steam engine in 1813. It had two legs at the back to make it go along. It blew up, killing fourteen people and injuring another forty-three. The idea did not catch on after that.

- That the first recorded steam railway death (that is, a man being run down by a locomotive) was on 5 December 1821. A carpenter named David Brook was walking home from Leeds along the line of the Middleton Railway in a blinding shower of sleet. He did not see or hear the train coming until it was too late.

- That the speed record for building an entire steam engine is held by the Great Eastern Railway. In 1891 they built a tank engine in just 9 hours, 57 minutes (including a first coat of paint). It was run straight afterwards and stayed in service until 1935.

- That, until the Channel Tunnel got built, Britain's longest railway tunnel was the one under the River Severn. It was opened in 1886 by the Great Western Railway to shorten the journey to the West Country and Wales. It took fourteen years to make and is 7 kilometres long (only 2 kilometres of it is under the river at any time).

- That a railway under the English Channel is not a new idea. In 1882, over a hundred years ago, plans were made for the Great Central Railway. This would run from the north of England, through London, under the Channel and join up with the railways in France and the rest of Europe. A start was made on digging the tunnel, but then permission for it was refused. The government (and the army) were afraid that the French might use the tunnel to invade Britain!

- That the only railway that ever had to carry a lifeboat and lifebelts was the Brighton & Rottingdean Seashore Electric Tramroad. It ran along

No. 777 *Sir Lamiel*. Built in 1925, this was one of seventy-four King Arthur Class locomotives built between 1919 and 1926, and the only one to survive. It went into service on the London & South Western Railway to replace older locomotives that were being overwhelmed by ever-heavier trains. A number of serious faults were found on some of the class, due to the builders under-bidding to win the contract, and then cutting corners on the building. They needed a good deal of rebuilding. The class was fast (one was timed at 90 miles an hour) but rather unstable at speed. This engine is now part of the National Railway Museum collection and its permanent home is with the Grand Central Railway at Loughborough.

the beach and, at high water, its long 'legs' were under 15 feet of water. This weird machine ran from 1896 to 1901.

- That Brunel was a brilliant railway designer, but hopeless at designing locomotives. He laid down strict rules for the first batch of Great Western locomotives that made it impossible for them to work properly. He wanted his engines to be very light, for the pistons to work very slowly and the boilers to have very little steam pressure. His rules forced the engine makers to produce engines with tiny boilers and cylinders and huge driving wheels. They could not pull any weight of carriages, were slow and quickly ran out of steam. About the only good engine the Great Western owned in 1838 was *North Star*. It had been made for another company, and had not been designed to Brunel's rules.

- That the electric telegraph was slow to catch on with some railways because most of their signalmen could not read or write. That meant they could not send or take down telegraph messages.
- That steam power nearly took to the skies. In 1842 inventors William Henson and John Stringfellow drew up plans for an aerial steam carriage that would carry ten passengers for 1,000 miles, at speeds of up to 50 miles an hour. A model version of it actually flew, but they could not find anyone to pay for the building of the full-size version.

PICTURE GALLERY

WHERE DOES THE WATER GO?

One way of describing tank engines is by where they store their water. These engines have four different ways of doing it.

Pannier tank engines like this one leave room underneath the tanks for people to get in and work on the mechanics of the engine.

Above: No. 30585 LSWR 0298 Class: This is a London & South Western Railway **well tank** engine – one of its water tanks is below its front axle and the other below the cab footplate. It is one of two survivors from a class of engine built between 1863 and 1875. Most of them were withdrawn between 1888 and 1898. But three survived on the isolated Bodmin & Wadebridge Railway in Cornwall, because they could cope with the railway's tight bends. They stayed in service until 1962. When they were withdrawn, they were the oldest design of engine still in use on British Railways. This one still works today.

Opposite above: *Ring Haw*: An 0-6-0 **saddle tank** locomotive, built in Leeds in 1940 for use in a quarry. It spent its whole life there, before being sold to the North Norfolk Railway in 1970. Its water is in a tank wrapped round the top of the boiler. Saddle tanks tend to be top-heavy and unstable at speed.

Opposite below: No. 4144 – Built at Swindon in 1946, this is a **side tank** engine and was one of a series of classes used to haul suburban services until its withdrawal in March 1965. It is now at the Didcot Railway Centre.

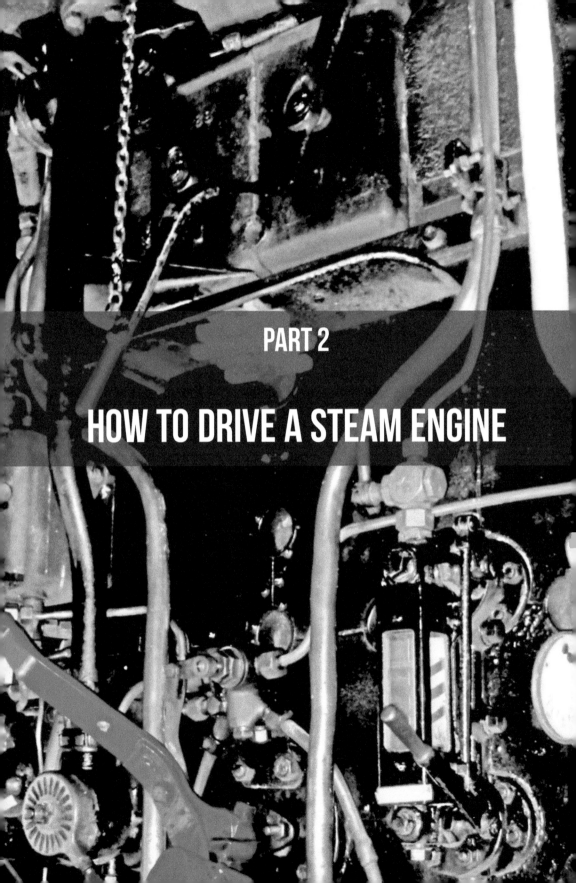

PART 2

HOW TO DRIVE A STEAM ENGINE

CHAPTER 6

HOW A STEAM ENGINE WORKS

Before we start to drive a steam engine, you need to understand how a steam engine works. And, before we look at that, you need to know something about steam. Steam is made by heating up water, but steam takes up a lot more space than the water from which it is made – about 1,500 times as much space. So a jug of water might make enough steam to fill a whole room. If that steam is not allowed to spread out – say, if water is heated to make steam in a sealed container – it presses against the sides of the container, as it tries to take up more space. It is this pressure that is used to make a steam locomotive move.

Put very simply, a steam locomotive has five main parts (see the diagram on the next page):

- a **firebox** (1), where the coal is burned to make heat. It is surrounded by:
- a large **boiler** (2), filled with water and with many small pipes running through it. The water in it is heated by the fire to make steam;
- **cylinders** (3) with pistons in them, which work rather like a giant bicycle pump. The steam is used to push the piston first one way, then the other;
- the pistons are joined to the wheels of the locomotive by **connecting rods** (4). These turn the in-and-out movement of the piston (called reciprocating movement) into the round-and-round movement of the locomotive's wheels, making it move along;
- a **smokebox** (5), where the used-up steam and the smoke from the fire are blown out through the chimney, sucking the heat from the firebox through the boiler tubes as it goes.

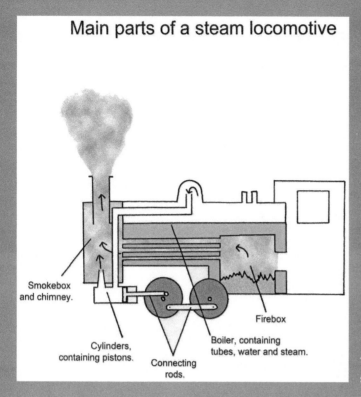

Main parts of a steam locomotive

Smokebox and chimney.

Cylinders, containing pistons.

Connecting rods.

Firebox

Boiler, containing tubes, water and steam.

The main parts of a steam locomotive.

Let's look at how this works in a little more detail. The firebox is surrounded by the boiler, so some of its heat goes straight from the firebox into the water, and starts heating it to make steam. More of the hot gases from the firebox go through the series of metal tubes that run from the firebox through the boiler and into the smokebox (I have just shown three tubes on my diagram, to make it easier to read, but there are really a lot more). This heats more water to make more steam. All that steam rises to the top of the boiler.

From the top of the boiler the steam goes down pipes into metal tubes, which are called the cylinders. Sometimes these cylinders can be seen on either side of the locomotive, in front of the big driving wheels. Sometimes they are underneath the boiler, and not so easy to see. A piston fits tightly inside each cylinder and the pressure of the steam is used to push the piston along the cylinder. At a certain point, the steam is stopped from pushing the piston in one direction and is let into the other side of the piston, to push it in the other direction. Locomotives will have at least two cylinders and they will always be slightly out of step with each other. This means that one of the cylinders is always able to push, to start the engine moving.

The connecting rods, which join the pistons to the locomotive's wheels, turn the in-and-out movement of the piston into the round-and-round movement of the wheels. The piston can only push so far before it has to start moving in the opposite direction. Once the locomotive has been pushed into moving, it will tend to keep moving in the same direction (this is called 'momentum'). The steam inside the cylinder is then switched from one side of the piston to the other. The piston is now being pushed back into the cylinder, rather than out of it, but it is still making the wheels go forward. These changes in direction of the piston, as the used steam is let out of the cylinder, make the chuffing noise that is the sound of a steam locomotive.

On many locomotives you can see a complicated set of rods and levers next to the cylinders. These are called the **valve gear**. All locomotives have some kind of valve gear, although sometimes you cannot easily see it. It is the valve gear's job to open and close the cylinder valves at just the right moment, so that the steam goes to the correct side of the piston. At the same time it lets out the used-up steam from the other side of the piston, ready for the return stroke. The valve gear can be changed by the driver to

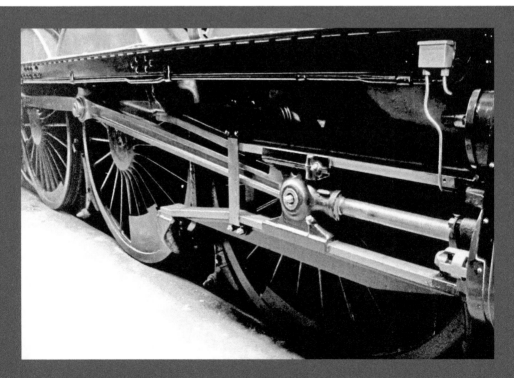

Stephenson valve gear on a Great Western locomotive.

make the engine run powerfully and efficiently. A good driver will try to give his engine as much steam as it needs to pull the train at the right speed, but no more, so that it uses as little coal and steam as possible. So, on a fast-running engine, it may only be necessary to let steam into the cylinder for a fifth of the piston stroke. The valve gear also makes it possible for the engine to go backwards.

The earliest type of valve gear to be widely used was invented in 1841 by two people who worked in Robert Stephenson's locomotive factory. It was called Stephenson valve gear, and was used on most British locomotives before 1900. Another type of valve gear was invented in 1844 by a Belgian engineer called Egide Walschaerts. But his took a long time to become popular and was not used in Britain until 1878. It later became much more popular, and many twentieth-century locomotives have Walschaerts valve gear – as does the first twenty-first century locomotive, *Tornado*.

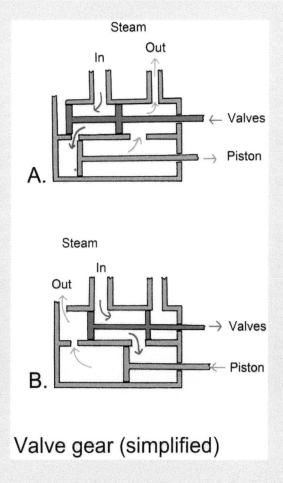

Valve gear (simplified)

How valve gear works.

The two diagrams on the opposite page show in a simple way how valve gear works. It takes a slice through the cylinder to see how the valves (shown in red) and the pistons (shown in green) work together to move the locomotive along. In the first picture (A), the valve rod is being pushed by the valve gear from right to left in our picture. This lets the fresh steam from the boiler (the dark-blue arrows) come into the left-hand side of the piston. At the same time, the used-up steam from the right-hand side of the piston (the light-blue arrows) is let out of the cylinder into the smokebox and up the chimney. The fresh steam then pushes the piston from left to right, driving the train's wheels around.

In the second picture (B), the piston has moved as far to the right as it can go and is ready to move back in the other direction. At this point the valve rod moves from left to right in our picture. This cuts off the supply of fresh steam to the left-hand side of the piston and opens up another valve. This lets out all the steam from the left-hand side – which has now done its job – and sends that used-up steam out into the smokebox and up the chimney. At the same time another valve opens up, which lets fresh steam into the right-hand side of the piston. It also closes off the escape route for the used-up steam from that side. This fresh steam can now push the piston from right to left, back to where we started.

The used-up steam from the cylinders is squirted at high speed into the smokebox. There it mixes with the hot gases from the fire that have just been sucked through the boiler. The gas and steam are blown out of the locomotive's chimney. The part of the engine that does this – the **blast pipe** – is explained in more detail shortly.

There is one other type of valve that has a special job to do. That is the safety valve, which normally sits on top of the boiler. It takes a lot of power to move a big engine and its carriages along the track, and that takes a lot of steam. The more steam the engine makes, the more that steam wants to expand – but it can't, as it is trapped inside the boiler. And what happens when steam can't expand? It builds up more pressure. Steam engine boilers are very strong, often built to take pressures of 200 pounds or more to every square inch, but sometimes the pressure could get too great even for them to bear. What could happen then is that the boiler might explode!

This would be like a bomb going off, shooting broken pieces of hot metal and boiling water everywhere. In the early days this used to happen from time to time, and people could be killed by it. To stop this happening, a special valve – a safety valve – was fitted to the boiler. If the steam pressure

A safety valve, doing its job.

in the boiler gets too high, it makes the safety valve work. Steam will come shooting out of it until the pressure inside the boiler becomes safe again and the safety valve can turn itself off. One of the reasons the boilers on the earliest engines sometimes used to explode was because foolish drivers used to tamper with their safety valves to stop them working. They hoped this would make their engines go faster, but sometimes it just made them go BANG! No driver would do that today.

These are just the basics of how steam locomotives work. Over the years many improvements have been made to their design. Take Stephenson's *Rocket* as an early example. *Rocket* had several new ideas, which were used on most of the engines that followed it.

A multi-tube boiler: most of the earliest steam engine designs had a single large tube, carrying the heat from the firebox through the boiler, heating the water as it went. Instead, *Rocket* had twenty-five small tubes. This meant that a lot more of the heat from the fire came into close contact with the water in the boiler, and this made more steam. This idea was invented by a Frenchman, Marc Seguin, although several different other people also claim it was their idea.

A blast pipe: once the steam had been used up, making the pistons move, *Rocket* sent it through a blast pipe, up the chimney along with the waste smoke from the fire. The steam went up through the smokebox at high speed, due to the narrow opening of the blast pipe. This created a vacuum. The vacuum sucked more hot air from the fire through the boiler tubes, and made the fire in the firebox burn more strongly. The original idea for this blast pipe may have come not from the Stephensons, but from Richard Trevithick, the designer of the Penydarren locomotive described in Chapter 1. The blast pipe idea worked best with a multi-tube boiler. With a single large tube, the blast pipe sucked too strongly, and blew not just smoke but also large bits of the fire straight out of the chimney. This meant the engine used up a lot more coal. It was also more likely to set fire to the rest of the train, or to the countryside or buildings near to the railway!

The blast pipe is important for a steam locomotive because of the way locomotives have to be designed. The easiest way to build a boiler would be with the tubes and the boiler above the firebox, because the hot gases from the fire will naturally want to rise up that way. But a boiler like this on a locomotive would be far too tall to fit through the tunnels and under the bridges you find on a railway. Instead, the boiler has to be in front of the firebox, with the tubes running horizontally through it, towards the front of the locomotive. The trouble is that the hot gases do not naturally want to go horizontally. Left to their own devices, the smoke and flames from the fire would come shooting out of the firebox door. This would not heat the water, but it could set fire to the driver and fireman! However the blast pipe sucks the hot air through the boiler tubes and out through the chimney, making good use of its heat as it goes.

A separate firebox: the hottest place on a steam engine (and so the best place to turn water into steam) was right next to the firebox. *Rocket*'s firebox had a double wall, and water from the boiler could run between the two walls. This meant the water was right up against the fire and could be heated more quickly.

Vertical and horizontal cylinders: Some of the earliest engines had vertical cylinders pushing the wheels around. This made the engine sway as it went along. High speeds would have been impossible with vertical cylinders. The locomotive would probably have fallen over! *Rocket* had its cylinders halfway between vertical and horizontal. This was better, but the best arrangement for smooth running was to have the cylinders nearly horizontal. Locomotives like *Planet,* built for the Liverpool & Manchester Railway in 1830, had horizontal cylinders. Within a few years, *Rocket* was also altered to have cylinders that were as near as possible to horizontal.

Two other improvements

I will just mention two other improvements made to locomotives, long after the days of the *Rocket.*

Superheated steam: Steam that goes from the boiler direct to the cylinders is called **saturated steam**. It still has water in it. Better use can be made of the steam by means of a process called **superheating**. This turns the water in the saturated steam into more steam. It means a given size of boiler can develop up to a quarter more power. (Or, to put it another way, it could develop the same power while using less fuel.)

   It works by passing the saturated steam through some very small tubes inside some of the boiler tubes. The temperature of this superheated steam can reach as much as 800 degrees Fahrenheit. The idea of superheating first appeared in 1841, but it took nearly fifty years before engine designers worked out how to cope with the pressures involved. But by 1913 the Great Western Railway alone had 750 superheated locomotives, saving them 15 per cent on their annual coal bill.

Compounding involves using the same steam twice, first in a high-pressure cylinder and then in a low-pressure one. This gives an extra 10–15 per cent of power, compared with a standard locomotive. The compounding system also puts less strain on the mechanical parts of the engine, although compound engines cost more to build and maintain. They were rare in Britain.

Coal and water; two essential things for making a steam engine go. The top of this building is a huge tank of water, supplying all the locomotives on the Didcot site. Below it is the coal store, from where coal can be tipped straight into the engines' bunkers or tenders.

Steam engines before steam locomotives

From their start in 1804, steam locomotives have used steam under pressure, but there were steam engines for a long time before 1804, even though nobody knew how to build engines that could work with high pressures. So the earliest steam engines worked in a different way.

We looked in Chapter 1 at the steam engines before the days of railways. As we saw, Thomas Newcomen invented a steam engine for pumping water out of mines, so that they would be safe for miners to work in. His machine was called an **atmospheric engine**. To explain how that works we need to look at what goes on in the air all around us.

You know when you get into a swimming pool and try to walk through it, it is harder than walking on dry land. That is because the water is pressing against you. The same is still happening even when you get out of the swimming pool. Everywhere we go there is air all around us, and that air is pushing against us in all directions. We call this air pressure and normally we don't notice it, because we are strong enough to push against it fairly easily.

But what would happen if there was somewhere that had no air in it at all? A space with no air or anything else in it is called a **vacuum**. What would the air around a vacuum do? It would try to rush into where the vacuum was to fill the gap. What Newcomen's engine did was to fill a cylinder with steam. That cylinder had a piston inside it that could go up and down inside the cylinder. When the cylinder was full of steam and it had pushed the piston to the top of the cylinder, Newcomen's engine would squirt cold water into the bottom of the cylinder.

When you mix cold water and steam, the steam turns back into water. As you will remember, steam takes up about 1,500 times as much space as water. So, before we had a cylinder full of steam, pressing against the sides to get out – now suddenly we have a cylinder containing a little bit of water, and a lot of nothing – Newcomen had made a vacuum. The air would try to

This odd-looking locomotive was nicknamed either the Hush-Hush or the Galloping Sausage (it never got an official name). It was designed by Sir Nigel Gresley and built in 1929. It contained a lot of new ideas, notably a boiler that worked at more than twice the pressure of normal locomotives – 450 pounds per square inch. But it was never really successful. It was rebuilt as a more conventional engine in 1936 and scrapped in 1959.

get in to fill the space. But it couldn't, because there was no way for it to get in past the piston. So, instead, the air pressure pushed down on the piston and moved it down the cylinder.

When the piston had been pushed right down, the engine would let the little bit of water in the cylinder out, and fill it again with steam. The pressure of the steam would push the piston back up to the top of the cylinder, and you would be back to the start of the process. The piston's up and down movements were connected to one end of a beam, which rocked up and down like a seesaw. This worked a pump, which sucked the water out of the mine.

So this was the first steam engine of modern times, but it was very slow and not very powerful. Other men – like John Smeaton and James Watt – later made it more powerful and faster. However, atmospheric engines would always be too heavy, too slow and too weak to power a steam railway locomotive.

No. 34070 *Manston* was part of the Southern region's Battle of Britain and West Country classes. 110 were built between 1945 and 1950 (*Manston* was built in 1947). They were mixed-traffic engines, powerful but light enough in weight to be able to run on tracks that had been neglected during the war years. Their unusual bodywork (it is called air smoothing, not streamlining) earned them the nickname 'spam cans'. They were good locomotives in many ways, but suffered from maintenance problems (they had many experimental parts). The class remained in service until July 1967, when the last Southern Region steam services were withdrawn. Twenty of these locomotives survive in heritage railways.

CHAPTER 7

HOW TO DRIVE A STEAM ENGINE

First steps

Now that you know how a steam engine works, the next step is to learn how to drive one. Driving a steam engine is a very skilled job and takes many years to learn, but this chapter of the book should give you a start.

The usual way to become an engine driver is to start as an engine cleaner. There you will learn a lot about how a steam engine works and how to get them ready for use. Then you would learn how to become a fireman. This is also a very skilled job in itself. You learn it as you do the job, by following what the engine driver teaches you.

Making just the right kind of fire takes a lot of experience. You have to give it the right amount of coal and air, and think about conditions on the track up ahead (if you know the line you are travelling on). Say you were coming towards a hilly section of track, or one where you wanted to go faster. This means that the engine will soon have to work harder, so you will need to make sure it has enough steam ready. Get that wrong, and you could run out of steam halfway up a hill.

A good fireman will see if one part of the fire is burning less brightly than another and will correct it. Even the coal you have to burn can vary in quality or size, and this may affect how you make the fire. Lastly, different types of engine have to be fired in different ways. They are like living things, each with their own character. A good fireman will find out how to get the best out of all the engines on which he works.

There are many other secrets to keeping the perfect fire. It is not just a question of putting as much coal on the fire as you can, for this increases the engine's running costs and can also make a lot of black smoke. 'Little and often' is the best way to add coal to the fire. The fireman will also be on guard against blowback. This is where the flames from the fire come shooting out of the firebox door onto the footplate and anyone standing nearby. I will explain what to do about that later. Last but not least, the fireman will also keep an eye on what is happening in the boiler – how are the steam pressure and the water level?

Once you are experienced as a fireman, you can think about learning to be a driver. The driver is the head of the team, and is responsible for the locomotive and its crew. However, we are going to take a shortcut in your training and – with the help of this chapter – you will be the driver of our imaginary steam engine.

The complicated controls of a Great Western express locomotive.

In the cab

When you climb into the cab of a steam engine, you will be faced by a confusing lot of small wheels, handles, dials, pipes and levers. These next sections tell you what the main ones are called, and what they do. Before 1948, the Great Western was the only one of the big railway companies to have a standard layout of the controls for all of its locomotives. That meant a Great Western driver could step into any of their engines and feel at home. Other companies' engines could vary in their layout, one from another. After the government took over the railways in 1948, they also had a standard layout for the footplate of any new engines they built – but it was not the same as the Great Western layout, which was the other way around.

So the controls on your engine may not be in exactly the same position as on our diagram, but your steam engine should have them all somewhere. Your first job as a driver on a locomotive that is new to you is to find out where they all are. The driver would have a little seat on the left-hand side

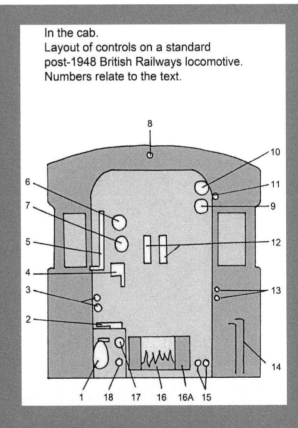

In the cab.
Layout of controls on a standard post-1948 British Railways locomotive. Numbers relate to the text.

Cab: layout of controls.

of the cab while the fireman's seat would be on the right (not that they have much time to sit down!). They each had a window to look out of; but, with a long steam engine in front of you, you could not see very much. This made it hard to see signals and the track ahead, especially if smoke from yours and other engines was blocking the view, so you have to look out carefully.

The next few paragraphs describe what the controls do, starting at the bottom left of the footplate – somewhere near where the driver's feet would be – and go round clockwise. This order is based on how British Railways arranged their engines that were built after 1948. This and the diagram on the previous page should help you find your way around these types of locomotives.

The controls

1. Reverser: This controls which side of the piston gets steam when the regulator is opened, and for how long it gets that steam. When you are starting off, the reverser is turned as far clockwise as it will go. This lets steam into the piston for about three-quarters of the piston's movement, pushing the engine strongly to get it moving forward. As the engine gets moving, less effort is needed. The reverser can gradually be turned anti-clockwise, letting less steam in. At its mid-position, no steam is being let into the cylinders. If you turn the reverser fully anti-clockwise, it lets steam into the other side of the piston and makes the engine go backwards.

2. Brake controller: There are three types of brakes on steam railway engines. They all work by pressing a brake block against the outer rim of the wheel to slow it down, rather like a bicycle brake. One uses air pressure to do this, one uses a vacuum and one uses steam. One or two of the very earliest locomotives had no brakes at all! On most of the early trains, only the locomotive had brakes and some had brakes just on the tender. This had to slow down the whole train. This could take a long time and made early trains rather dangerous. Normal stops had to be planned a long way in advance. Emergency stops could not be planned, but still took a long time! Some slow-moving historic goods trains may still work this way, except that they would have an extra handbrake in the guard's van at the back of the train. But all passenger trains now have to have **continuous brakes** on all their carriages, so every carriage helps the train to stop. These brakes

also come on automatically if one part of the train gets separated from the rest.

On trains with air brakes, the locomotive pumps air to all the train's carriages or wagons through the pipes that join them together. As the brake pipes are put under pressure, it pushes the pistons into the brake cylinders. This turns the brakes off and leaves the train free to move. When the driver puts the brakes on, the brake lever reduces the pressure in the brake pipes. This causes the brakes to come on and stops the train. The brake controller gives the driver control over the amount of air pressure there is in the brake pipes. This will decide how hard the brakes will come on. Even today, the brakes on a train need to go on fairly gently. If they go on too hard, the wheels will just lock, the train will skid along the tracks, the wheels could get damaged and the passengers could be in for a rough ride!

3. Ejector valves: On a train with vacuum brakes, the engine has to create the vacuum that makes them work. This is done using the ejector valves. These shoot high-pressure steam through a cone and out through the chimney. The opening of this cone sits in the middle of a pipe leading to the train-brake pipe. As the steam squirts out at high speed, it sucks all the air out of the train-brake pipe, creating the vacuum. There is a one-way valve on the brake pipe, so the air can be sucked out of it but cannot get back in again. As long as there is a vacuum in the brake pipes, the brakes are off and the engine is ready to roll. The only way air can get back into the pipe is if the driver puts the brake lever on. This lets air into the pipes and puts the brakes on, stopping the train.

4. Brake valve: This is the lever that puts the brakes on.

5. Regulator: This lever connects to a valve that controls the amount of steam going from the boiler to the cylinders. It, and the valve gear, work like the accelerator on a car, making the engine go faster or slower.

6. Steam chest pressure gauge: The steam chest is a space in, or just on top of, the cylinders. It is where the steam is held after it comes from the boiler, and before it goes into the cylinders to drive the engine along. The steam chest pressure gauge tells you how much pressure there is in that steam. Is there enough to allow the engine to go at the speed you want it to? Or maybe there is too much pressure – in which case you might need to close the regulator a little.

7. Brake gauge: The brake gauge tells you how much power there is in the train's brakes – how much air pressure or how much of a vacuum, depending on the type of brakes. Will you be able to stop the train when you need to, and how quickly will it be able to stop?

8. Manifold isolation valve: The manifold collects the steam from the top of the boiler and sends it to the cylinders and wherever else it needs to go. On older locomotives, the steam was collected in a dome on top of the boiler, like the one shown in our diagram of the main parts of a steam engine;

9. Main boiler pressure gauge: This tells you the pressure of the steam in the main boiler. If it is too high, some of the things you might do include putting some more cold water into the boiler to take some of the steam away, closing the dampers to make the fire produce less steam, or opening the regulator more to use up some of the steam by going faster. If the pressure is too low, you might close the regulator a little to use less steam, open the dampers or stoke up the fire to make more steam;

10. Steam-heating pressure gauge: Older carriages are heated by feeding steam from the engine through pipes in the carriages to heat radiators under the seats. The longer the train is, the more steam pressure is needed to heat them all, and the harder it is to get it right. What can happen is that the people in the front carriage get roasted, while those in the last carriage freeze. The gauge tells the driver how high the pressure in the heating pipes is, and the engine may have a scale showing how much pressure is needed to keep each carriage warm.

11. Steam heating valve: This is how the driver controls the amount of steam going to heat the carriages;

12. Boiler water gauges: Many engines have two of these, but Great Western engines have just one. This glass tube tells you how much water you have in the boiler. The stripes behind it make it easier to see the water level, since the water in the gauge glass makes the stripes seem to change direction. (This is called **diffraction**.) The gauge can give false readings if, for example, the top cock (the lever at the top of the gauge) is not fully open, or the pipes taking water to the gauge get blocked up. Also, if the engine is going up a slope, the gauge might give you a higher reading than the real one; if it is going downhill, the reading might tend to be too low.

Getting (and keeping) the right water level in the boiler is vital. If it gets too low the firebox could overheat and even melt. As a safety measure, fireboxes have a metal plug (called a fusible plug) in them. This is designed to melt first if the firebox starts overheating, letting water onto the fire. If the water level gets too high, there is not enough room in the boiler for steam to collect, and there is also a danger of something called **priming** – where water instead of steam gets into the cylinders and damages them. You should aim always to keep your glass at least half full;

13. Steam injector valves: The water in the boiler is under pressure when the engine is running. So, if you need to put more water into the boiler, it will not just run in by itself. It needs to be pushed in under pressure. The steam injector valves push the water into the boiler. There are live steam injectors, which use steam straight from the boiler to do the pushing. But when the engine is running and the regulator is open, you can use the exhaust steam that has just been through the cylinder to do the same job. This makes better use of your steam and means you burn less coal. When the train is standing still and there is no exhaust steam, a back-up supply of steam from the boiler automatically takes over and does the job. Just a few engines will have a mechanical pump to push water into the boiler if you have no steam at all to work the injectors.

    These injectors are very important. As we saw, if the boiler runs short of water, the firebox plug could melt and damage the boiler. It is also important that water can be injected into the boiler, but that the pressurised water in the boiler cannot push its way out again down that same pipe. So the injector pipe has a one-way valve called a clack valve that lets water into the boiler but does not let water or steam out again.

14. Injector water valves: These turn on the water supply from the tender or the engine's tank, ready to be injected into the boiler;

15. Damper handles: The dampers are flaps underneath the firebox, opened and closed by these handles. The dampers help control the amount of air going into the fire, and hence how strongly the fire burns. They are also opened after a journey to make it possible to clean out the ash that collects in the ashpan, under the fire;

16. Firebox and 16A Firebox doors: The firebox is where the fire burns that makes the steam. It has doors on it that can help control the amount of air reaching the fire and also protect the crew from blowback;

17. Blower: When the engine is not moving, there is no jet of used-up steam coming from the blast pipe, and so no draught to make the

fire burn better. The blower valve allows steam from the boiler to be squirted up the chimney so as to get the same effect as a blast pipe, and get the fire burning. It also helps protect the crew from blowback;

18. Sanders: If the rails get wet or icy, it may be difficult for the engine wheels to grip. The sanders sprinkle sand onto the top of the rail, just by the driving wheels, to help them grip. These work either by gravity or steam power. The driver will turn these on when needed;

And there are some other controls, not shown on our diagram:

19. Whistle: This does what its name says! Your whistle should be sounded before the engine starts to move, or if you are coming up to a level crossing, or anywhere where there may be people close to the line;
20. Lubricators: These feed a little oil into the pistons and cylinders to keep them lubricated while the engine is moving and the regulator is open. If the regulator is closed completely, the supply of oil stops, so it is important to keep the regulator slightly open, even when the engine is coasting. Without regular oiling, moving parts like the pistons could seize up inside the cylinders;
21. Cylinder drain cocks: Steam can condense, leaving water to gather in the cylinders. If it is left there and the engine is moved, it can damage the cylinders. The cylinder drain cocks blow that water out, making a lot of steam as the engine moves off;
22. Speedometer: Just like the speedometer in a car, it tells you how fast you are going. Many steam engines were not fitted with a speedometer until the 1950s. Before that, the drivers had to guess their speed;
23. Automatic Train Control: A safety control. If an engine passes a signal at danger, ATC automatically sounds a warning for the driver or puts the brakes on, if the driver does not do it himself.

Getting ready to go

So we have now seen the controls. What do we do now to get the engine started? A steam engine is not like a car. You cannot just jump in, turn a key and drive away. The driver, the fireman and cleaners need to arrive many hours before the engine is due to go. The first jobs they have to do include:

- making sure that the engine has enough coal and water, and that there is sand in the sandboxes;
- making sure the water gauges are working;
- checking the firebox for leaks or damage;
- opening the smokebox to check for signs of water or steam leakage;
- cleaning out what is left of the previous fire;
- starting the new fire with scraps of wood and old rags;
- gradually building up the new fire with coal;
- cleaning the fittings with brass cleaner and polishing the paintwork;
- checking for loose pins or other faults in the moving parts, fixing them and then cleaning them;
- wiping all the lubrication points and giving them any grease or oil that they need. (A large locomotive might have 100 or more places needing lubrication);
- taking the boiler up to full pressure and letting it blow off steam to make sure the safety valves are working;
- testing all the valves and other working parts to make sure they are in good order.

Getting started

Back in 1947, the London Midland & Scottish Railway put out a poster about how to drive a steam engine. According to them, it could not be easier! There were just four steps to starting:

- Put the reversing gear into 'forward';
- Set the brake handle to 'off';
- Adjust the ejectors to create a vacuum for the brakes; and
- Open the regulator slightly.

Stopping was even easier – with only three steps!

- Close the regulator;
- Put the reversing lever into the middle 'drift' position;
- Apply the brake.

In fact, it is much more complicated than that. Your list of things to do at the start might be more like this:

- Make sure the cylinder cocks are open to blow out any water that has collected in the cylinders;
- Check that the handbrake (on the tender of a tender locomotive) is on;
- Look for the signal to go from your guard or shunter;
- Put the reverser into 'forward' (unless you want to go backwards!);
- Shut the driver's air admission valve (on vacuum brakes);
- Use the blower to get the fire burning strongly until the train is moving;
- Make sure the brakes are in working order, and are 'off';
- Release the handbrake;
- Open the ejector to create a vacuum to release the brakes;
- Once the brake vacuum has reached 25 inches of mercury (other locomotives may require 22 inches), look back along the train and make sure that all the doors are shut correctly and everyone is on board;
- If they are on, turn the injectors off;
- Look ahead to make sure the signals say it is safe to start;
- Sound your whistle to show you are about to start;
- Gently open the regulator, allowing time for the pressure to build up in the cylinders;
- Once the train has moved a couple of coach lengths, shut the cylinder cocks, keeping an eye on the exhaust from the chimney in case too much water from the boiler is coming out;
- Continue to open the regulator gently as the train gathers speed;
- As you gather speed, turn down the blower and wind back the cut-off on the reverser to make more efficient use of your steam;
- Once you are up to speed, shut the brake ejector, as the vacuum pump should maintain the vacuum in the brake system;
- All the time as you go along, you will be looking ahead to make sure the signals say it is safe to continue, looking out for hazards along the track and making sure the dials are giving the right readings;
- As you approach your first stop, apply the brakes well in advance, in a series of gentle movements of the brake lever;
- As you come to a halt, put on the blower to avoid blowback and put the locomotive into mid-gear.

Meanwhile the fireman also has a lot of work to do:

- On a big engine he will be putting four to six shovelfuls of coal onto the fire every couple of minutes. On a long journey in a fast train, a fireman may have to throw several tons of coal into the firebox, so he needs to be fit and strong;
- He will be watching the flames from the fire. There should be a thin covering of coal over the whole fire, but it should not be allowed to burn right through so that you can see the metal bars in the firebox. Too thick a layer of coal can kill a fire, by not allowing enough air to go through it;
- In between shovelling, he will also be watching the smoke the engine is making. He will be aiming for a light-grey colour. If the smoke is dark, it means not all of the fuel in the coal is being burnt, which is a waste. If the smoke disappears completely, it is time to put more coal on the fire. The aim is to keep the train running on time, while using as little coal as possible;
- As the train comes into a station, the fireman will close the firebox doors to limit the air getting to the fire and also to protect against blowback. This will also help stop the engine making too much steam while it is not needed. Station stops are also a good time to inject more water into the boiler, using spare steam that might otherwise be wasted.

At the end of the day

You will normally leave a small fire in the engine firebox. This means the boiler will cool down gradually as the fire goes out. Make sure there is not too much ash in the ashpan, under the firebox. There will soon be more in there, as you 'clean out' the fire to remove any ash and clinker (clinker is ash that has turned into a solid block, and which can stop the fire burning properly). There are valves to put into their resting positions. Finally, close the dampers to limit the amount of air getting to the fire, so that it burns slowly. After all that, there may still be log books for the driver to fill in.

There are also jobs that need doing regularly on a locomotive. One of these is a **wash-out**. The water used in steam engines will probably have impurities in it. These collect in the boiler and form a nasty gooey sludge.

During a wash-out, the locomotive's boiler is emptied (when the engine is not in steam) and a powerful hose is used to wash away the sludge. Chemicals are also put in the engine's water tanks, so as to stop the sludge sticking to the boiler. A similar job to a wash-out may be done by a **blow-down**. This means letting some of the water out of the boiler through a special tap while the engine is in steam. Because the water is hot and under pressure, it comes shooting out very quickly, instantly turning into a lot of steam and carrying the sludge out with it. This needs to be done with great care!

PICTURE GALLERY

LOGOS

This is the original badge of the Great Western Railway, showing the crests of the cities of London and Bristol, the two ends of the company's first line.

This is the badge used by British Railways after they were taken over by the government in 1948. Some people call it the bicycling lion.

This is the new badge (or logo) they chose when British Railways decided to modernise and become British Rail in 1964. British Rail used it on everything until 1994, when the railways were sold back to private companies (privatised). You still see it on road signs and railway stations. Does it mean 'we don't know whether we are coming or going'?

DID YOU KNOW ...?

- That horses were last used to pull railway wagons more recently than you might think. The last railway horse, called Charlie, was still working in the goods yard at Newmarket moving wagons about until 1967. The last passenger railway service in England drawn by horses was the 'Port Carlisle Dandy' that ran along the Solway Firth in Cumbria until April 1914. Scotland had one until 1917, and one in Northern Ireland ran until 1957. It was three-quarters of a mile long and took 6 minutes.
- Why the world's fastest steam engine is called *Mallard*? Its designer, Sir Nigel Gresley, was a lover of wild birds, and mallards were one of the types of duck he kept on a pond at his home. A *Bittern* is also a type of duck.
- That *Mallard* cost £8,500 to build in 1937. *Tornado*, the first steam locomotive to be built in the twenty-first century, cost £3,000,000.
- That the A4 Pacific *Bittern* has spent part of its life pretending to be other locomotives? It was repainted and re-badged to look like *Silver Link* (the first A4 Pacific) for an event in York in 1988. In 2010 it impersonated *Dominion of New Zealand*. Both of these were A4 Pacifics that had been scrapped. In 2008 it even impersonated *Spencer*, one of the characters from the *Thomas the Tank Engine* books.
- That the longest platform in Britain is at Gloucester. It is 602.6 metres long – more than six football pitches. That is, unless you live in Colchester, where some people claim theirs is 620 metres long. Or people from Manchester will tell you that when they joined up their Victoria and

Exchange stations it gave them a platform 646 metres long. Take your pick! But they are all well behind Chicago, in America, whose station has a platform 1,066 metres long – that's about two-thirds of a mile!

- That there are code letters on some locomotives that tell you about what they do. There are numbers to tell you how powerful they are (they go from 0 to 8 for passenger engines and 0 to 9 for freight engines – 0 is the least powerful and 8/9 the most powerful). Then there are code letters to tell you what kinds of trains they pull – P for passenger, F for freight or, if they pull both types, it might say PF, or MT for mixed traffic.

- That George Churchward of the Great Western, one of the most famous of locomotive designers, was killed by an express train while crossing the main line in 1933.

- That in 1910 the North British Locomotive Company built a steam engine that used its steam power to drive the electric motors that made it move. It was not a success and only one was ever built. Armstrong-Whitworth tried something similar in 1922, with an equal lack of success. But in 1935 the LMS built a successful locomotive – called *Turbomotive* – in which the steam powered a turbine, instead of cylinders, to move it.

- That in 1925 the GWR and the LNER swapped express locomotives to see which was best – GWR's 4-6-0 *Pendennis Castle* or LNER's 4-6-2 *Victor Wild*. *Pendennis Castle* was the clear winner, being both quicker and more economical.

- That during the Second World War a steam engine brought down a German warplane. On 28 November 1942 a Southern Railway train was going across Romney Marsh, when the plane dived down and machine-gunned it. As the plane flew over the locomotive, its boiler exploded. It blew the plane out of the sky, killing its pilot.

- That the most powerful steam locomotive ever to run on British lines was the LNER's U1 Class articulated engine, with its 2-8-0+0-8-2 wheel arrangement. Introduced in 1925, it was 87 feet long and was used for pulling heavy coal trains over the steep Woodhead route. It was fitted with gas masks for the crew to wear while going through tunnels on this route. It was withdrawn in 1955.

- That a double-decker train used to run on Britain's railways. It started work on the Southern Region's Dartford line on 2 November 1949. Because it could take more people it had to wait longer at stations to load or unload, so there was no advantage to it. It was withdrawn in October 1971.
- That the fastest a steam train travelled on Britain's main-line railways, during the age of steam after the Second World War, was 112 miles an hour. This was done in 1959 by one of Gresley's A4 Pacifics.
- That every mile of track on British Rail has between 2,124 to 2,479 sleepers, and that the track can carry loads of up to 25 tons on each axle. Modern sleepers tend to be made of concrete. They last from

No. 31806. This U Class locomotive started life as something rather different – a K Class tank engine. The K Class was known to be unstable if the tracks were at all rough and, after one of them came off the tracks at Sevenoaks in 1927, killing thirteen people, the order was given for them all to be converted to U class tender engines. No. 31806 was one of these, and entered service in 1928. The conversion was successful and the class remained in service until 1966. Four examples survive on different heritage railways, this one on the Swanage Railway.

forty to fifty years, about twice as long as the old wooden ones, and weigh more than twice as much (about 267 kilograms).

- That the first preserved railway in Britain was the Festiniog, in Wales. Its original job was carrying slates, but this stopped in 1946. The Festiniog Society was formed in 1954 and they started running passenger services on 23 July 1955.
- That possibly the largest steam engine ever built was the Ya01, built in Britain in 1932 for the Russian Railway. It stood 17 feet high and weighed 262.5 tons. Its wheel arrangement was 2-8-2 plus 2-8-4.
- That one of the oldest surviving railway engines is also one of the most famous railway engine film stars. *Lion* was built for the Liverpool & Manchester Railway in 1838, and has starred in three films. In one, *The Titfield Thunderbolt*, made in 1952, it really was the central character.
- That the last British Railways branch line to be operated by steam was between Brockenhurst and Lymington, which stopped being steam-hauled on 30 March 1967.
- That Britain's worst railway disaster occurred at Quintinshill, near Gretna Green in Scotland, on 22 May 1915. A train full of soldiers, heading south to be sent off to the battlefield of Gallipoli, collided with a stationary local train. A moment later, a northbound express sleeper train crashed into the wreckage. The carriages were wooden and lit by gas, and they all caught fire. 226 people, mostly soldiers, were killed and 246 injured. The signalmen, who took the blame for the disaster, were sent to prison.
- That Britain's oddest railway accident might well be one in Swinton on 28 April 1953. A railway tunnel had been dug underneath a filled-in mineshaft. On this day the filled-in shaft collapsed onto the tunnel, and two houses that had been built on top of it collapsed into the shaft. Five people were killed.
- Another freak railway accident happened at Waterloo on the Southern Railway in 1904. A man was doing some repairs at the side of the track when he accidentally stepped on a wire that worked a signal. It turned the signal from 'stop' to 'go', and led to a collision between a milk train and a passenger train, in which a passenger was killed.
- That in 1931 the LMS tried out a bus that would run on road or rail. It would do 60 miles an hour on the road and 70 miles an hour on rail, but it was not successful and was scrapped after a few years.

PART 3

RUNNING A STEAM RAILWAY

CHAPTER 8

WHO'S STEERING? SIGNALS, POINTS AND SAFETY

Can your train use the line? Loading gauge and weight limits

Before you even begin your journey, you need to know that your train can pass safely along the route. There are two things to check.

The loading gauge sets the size limits (height and width) for any engine, carriage or wagon going along a particular length of railway line. It makes sure your train will not bump into any bridge, tunnel, station platform or anything else along the line. In the days when open goods wagons were used, stations used to have a type of measure – a loading gauge – over the rails at the exit of the railway yard. This made sure wagons were not loaded too high to pass safely along the line. Because Britain built some of the earliest railways, our loading gauges tended to be smaller than in most other countries.

A train that wants to be able to go anywhere on the British main line should be no greater than 12 feet, 8 inches high and 8 feet, 10 inches wide. But different railway companies had different loading gauges. Most lines are at least 13 feet by 9 feet. The Great Western (which was originally built to take broad-gauge trains) is bigger – 13 feet, 6 inches by 9 feet, 8 inches.

Many European railways are bigger even than this, and their trains cannot run on British lines. This is more of a problem now that we have the Channel Tunnel. The tunnel's loading gauge is 17 feet, 8.5 inches by 13 feet, 1.5 inches, so trains from Europe can at least enter Britain. New lines, linking Britain to Europe and carrying European trains, have to be built to that bigger gauge.

The other thing that may limit where a train can go is its weight. Different tracks and bridges are built to take different weights of traffic – a branch line may not be able to support heavy locomotives that could happily run on main lines. Weight is measured according to the load on each axle. Modern diesel trains are built to have a maximum axle weight of about 19 tons per axle (so that is up to 77 tons for a four-axle locomotive, or 114 tons for one with six axles). Each route on the modern railway has a Route Availability score, which says how much axle weight it can take. So an RA3 line can take up to 16.5 tons, while an RA10 (the strongest) can take up to 25.4 tons.

There are also things called light railways. They are built to lower standards than normal railways (for example, fewer sleepers, steeper hills, tighter bends). They are easier to get permitted and cheaper to build, but may also be subject to different limits, such as lower speed limits or weight limits. A number of preserved steam railways run on light railway lines.

The Great Western built a steam locomotive called the *Great Bear* in 1908. It was the first British locomotive with a 4-6-2 Pacific wheel arrangement and was the biggest engine in the country. It had an axle loading of 20 tons. At that time there was only one line in the whole of the Great Western network strong enough to take its weight. They did not build a second one and the *Great Bear* was scrapped in 1924.

Signals and safety

Railways had new safety problems that nobody had thought about before. First, they were far faster than any means of transport ever seen before. Even the early ones could go a lot faster than a galloping horse. Second, they were very bad at stopping. The brakes on early locomotives (if they had any) did not work well and they had a huge weight of carriages or trucks behind them that they had to stop. Metal wheels easily skidded on metal rails, so stopping had to be done gently. Lastly, unlike other transport, they could not swerve out of the way if they were about to collide with something. It took trains so long to stop that you could not rely on the driver seeing danger far enough ahead. Even a modern high-speed train, with modern brakes, takes a long time to stop from full speed. A different way of controlling trains was needed.

Modern railways have light signals, like the traffic lights we have on roads. On the other hand, steam railways have had different kinds of signals over the years. Some of the earliest railways did not have signals at all. Instead, every mile or so along the railway, there would be a little hut by the tracks with a man inside it. This hut was called a **police station** and the man was called a **policeman**. His main job was to tell the driver of each train that came along either that it was safe to carry on, or that the driver should carry on, but to be careful ('caution'), or that he should stop immediately. He did this by signals with his arms. The pictures show you how. At night, he would use coloured lamps to signal.

1. All clear.

2. Go ahead, but be careful.

3. STOP!

The railway policeman – the human signal, saying 'go ahead', 'caution' and 'stop'.

The only way the policeman knew whether it was safe for the train to go ahead was to look at his watch and see how many minutes it was since the last train went past. He would allow a certain number of minutes between each train (anywhere from 5 to 15 minutes). For example, a train arriving less than 5 minutes after the last one might be stopped. One arriving between 5 and 10 minutes after the last one might be told to go ahead, but with caution. One arriving after more than 10 minutes might just be told to go ahead. This was not a perfect system. For example, a train might break down or be slowed down by something after passing the policeman. Or a carriage or wagon might fall off the back of the previous train, and be left behind for the next train to crash into.

As trains got faster, it became more and more difficult for the drivers to see hand signals. Fixed mechanical signals started to be used instead. Some of these were rather odd; the signal outside Reading station in 1840 was a ball, and drivers were told not to enter the station if they could not see the ball. But how do you stop at a signal you cannot see? Another of

An early Great Western disc and crossbar signal.

Brunel's signals used a series of fans to send messages to the train. But these fans soon got torn to pieces by the wind, and became useless. The Great Western's disc and crossbar signals were some of the first to give a clear 'stop' or 'go ahead' signal.

However, most railways used the semaphore signal. These were first introduced in 1841 and you will still see these signals at most steam railways today. Some examples are shown in the picture. There are two main kinds of semaphore signal – the **stop** or **home** signal, which has a red arm with a white stripe, and **distant** signal, which is yellow with a 'V' cut out of the end and a black arrow painted on it.

With the home signal, if the arm is pointing either up or down (different railways had them pointing in different directions) it was safe to go. But if the arm was pointing straight out, the train had to stop at that signal. With the distant signal, the all-clear signal was the same, but the straight-out signal meant you could still go ahead, but be ready to stop at the next home signal.

At night, you could not see the arms, so lights were used instead. At one end of the arm of the signal, you will see two glasses (called spectacles). The spectacles on a stop signal were coloured red (for 'stop') and green (for 'go'). On a distant signal, the spectacles were yellow (for 'caution') and green (for 'go'). A light would shine through one or other of the glasses, depending on whether the signal was at 'stop' or 'go'. There are also combined stop and distant signals. They can give three kinds of message – 'stop', 'caution' or 'go'.

For safety, if for example the wire that worked the signal broke, there would be weights on the signal that made it fall into the 'stop' position. Semaphore signals were usually reliable, but not always perfect. In very bad weather they could get frozen in the wrong position. They could also jam halfway, making it difficult to see whether the signal was at 'stop' or 'go'.

There are some other types of semaphore signals that are sometimes used. They are called **permissive signals**. These control local movements of trains, rather than the movement of trains over longer distances from one block of track to another. These can give three types of instruction.

Calling-on is the most common type. This type of signal can be found under the stop signal controlling entry to a platform. It is like a stop signal but smaller, and its white stripe goes along the middle of the signal arm, rather than across it. It will have the letter 'C' on it. It allows either for two trains to share a platform, or for extra vehicles to be attached to a train, or for a locomotive to come in and be attached to some coaches already at the platform.

Shunt-ahead allows a train to shunt forward to get clear of some points (this signal has an 'S' on it).

Finally, there is a **warning** signal (with a letter 'W' on it), which allows a train to enter a section without it being safe to go right through it. This might be used to let a goods train get into a siding, while the station ahead still has a train stopped in it.

There are also **shunting signals**. Some of these take the form of a white disc with a red stripe across them, low on the ground. They work like a home signal. These control local movements into, out of and around goods yards.

Signalling might not be the only job a railwayman had to do. At small country stations, where only a few trains came through each day, it would not make sense to have someone employed all day just to work a few signals. So the station might have a porter/signalman, who loaded and unloaded goods trains and helped passengers with their luggage, as well as working the signals. They might even be responsible for looking after the

Can you spot the one distant signal among the home signals?

station gardens, as station staff took a great pride in their gardens. There were competitions, with prizes.

Exploding signals!

Fog creates special problems for railways. Drivers cannot see signals or lights. So, when the fog got bad, signalmen would be sent out to the distant signals, carrying lanterns and explosive charges called detonators. If the distant signal was on 'caution' (meaning that the home signal ahead was on 'stop'), the signalman would fix the detonators to the track. The weight of the train passing over them exploded them. The loud bang warned the driver to stop the train, even if he could not see the signal. If the distant signal was on 'go', the detonators would be taken off the rails and the signalman would wave a green lantern to let the train pass.

In 1906 the Great Western Railway introduced a new safety system called Automatic Train Control (ATC). This did away with the need for detonators. Each time a train came towards a signal at 'go', it would ring a bell in the driver's cab. If the signal was not at 'go', it would sound a warning horn in the cab. The driver then had to put the train's brakes on. If he did not do so quickly enough, the ATC would put the brakes on for him.

The Block system

It soon became clear that the time-interval system was not a safe enough system to protect trains. Trains went at very different speeds and could catch each other up between signals. Nor did it make the best use of the railway. If a ten-minute time interval was needed between trains, it meant that only six trains an hour could use the track. As the numbers of trains grew, the railway needed a safe way of reducing the time gap (called the **headway**) between them on busy lines.

What they came up with was the block system. This only applied to railways with two or more tracks, where each track was used by trains going in one direction only. Special rules apply to single-track lines and we will look at them later. The block system meant that only one train could be in any **block section** at any time. A block section was a length of railway running from the last stop signal controlled by the previous signal box, to the first stop signal controlled by the next signal box. Each signal box controls a distant signal and one or more stop (or home) signals. The distant signal is the first one the driver will see as he enters a new block section. If the distant signal is at 'go', it means that all the signals controlled by that signal box should also be at 'go'. If it is telling him to be ready to stop, the driver will know that this distant signal is far enough ahead of the next home signal for him to be able to stop.

The block system works by a signal box (call it box A) 'offering' a train passing through their section to the next signal box along the line (box B). If their line is clear, box B can 'accept' the train. If the line is not clear, box B can refuse the train and it will be stopped. As the train passes each signal box, the signalman will look to see whether the last wagon or carriage has a red tail lamp on it. This shows him that no wagons or carriages have fallen off the back of the train. He will then offer the train to the next block of track (box C).

The signal boxes 'talk' to each other by ringing electric bells in each other's signal box. They use a code – so, for example, two rings means 'train entering section'. All the bell signals that are sent or received are written down in a big book called the Train Register, which also keeps a record of any incidents that occur.

Single-line working

So far we have seen how railways work when there are two or more lines, and where each line only carries trains going in one direction. New problems arise when there is only a single line, carrying trains in both directions. The most obvious one is that two trains might be heading in opposite directions towards each other along the same length of track, not knowing that the other train is there. The simplest solution to this is to let only one engine use the track at a time, so that there is nothing for them to crash into. This is called **one engine in steam.** It is the way some single-line steam railways and goods-only lines work today, but it is not always possible.

Another solution is a **token** system. With this, there is a single object that gives you the right to go along a section of single-line track. Unless the driver has this object in his hand, he cannot enter that section of track. When he gets to the other end, he has to give it up for the next driver to use. This token can be all sorts of things – a key, a metal plate called a tablet, or a

The fireman hands over the token at the end of a stretch of single-line working.

wooden staff with a brass plate on it, for example. In each case, it would say on it the length of track on which it could be used.

Where the token is something small, like a key, it is sometimes kept in a leather pouch, attached to a large hoop. The signalman would hold up the hoop as the train came to the start of the single-line section and the fireman would hook his arm through the hoop and take it from him as the train went past, without having to stop. At the end of the section the fireman would return the token to the next signalman in the same way. This avoided delay to the train.

This is fine, if the next train will be going the opposite way along the track, and can pick up the token at the other end. But what if several trains are going in the same direction, one after another? A different token system came into use for this. In this, the driver of the first train would be shown (but not given) the token. Instead he would be given a written permission (called a ticket) to enter the track. These tickets are numbered and kept in a locked box, the key to which is attached to the token. A written record is kept of every ticket given out. The token stays in that signal box, which means the signal box at the other end cannot let any trains through in the opposite direction.

Another system involved the use of electric token machines in signal boxes at either end of a single-line section, and linked to each other by telegraph. Each machine has a supply of tokens, but only one can be issued at a time, and even that is only given out if the signalmen at both ends of the single-track line agree. Once a token has been taken out, an extra one cannot be removed until the one that is 'out' has been replaced, in either machine. So only one token can be in use at any one time. Where two sections of single-line track are next door to each other, the tokens are of different designs, so they cannot be put in the wrong machine.

Steering, interlocking and safety

One control that a car has but a steam locomotive does not is a steering wheel. For the train driver does not steer the engine. That is done by the signalmen in their signal boxes. They pull the levers that direct the trains onto one line or another. In the earliest days of steam railways, each individual junction or point had its own pointsman, who controlled it with a lever. As a train approached, the pointsman had to know which line it was supposed to go down. To help tell the pointsman where a train was going, coloured symbols or lights could be put on the front of the engine.

The first signal box, from which all the signals and points for a stretch of railway could be controlled, was built on the London & Croydon Railway in 1844. Numbers of signal boxes started appearing from about 1863, when a company called Saxby and Farmer started making them. At first these were mechanical signal boxes, using cables and levers to move the points and signals. They could only control an area of a few hundred yards, else the levers became too hard to pull. Modern ones are electronic, and can work the points and signals over a much wider area. But quite a number of the old-style mechanical ones are still in use.

Switches or points – where two or more lines join – and crossings – where two or more lines cross each other, are very important parts of any railway track. They suffer more wear than other sections of the track, not least because some of them – the points – have moving rails. About three times as much is spent on maintaining them, compared with other parts of the track. Points also have problems with extreme temperatures. If they get too cold, they may stop working, so some in cold places are heated, or insulated to keep out the cold. They can also get too hot, so you may see lengths of track painted white. This reflects some of the heat from the sun and keeps them a little cooler. The third rail used to supply power to some electric trains can also get covered in ice and stop working.

One danger is that the signalman could set up a route for a train through his block, and set the signals and points to 'go'. Then he finds that another, conflicting route has been set up for another train and the signals for that are also at 'go'. The Victorians got around this by a safety feature called **interlocking**. This is a series of metal rods attached to the signal levers in the signal box. These lock the points in place, once they have been set, and prevent conflicting movements being set up. Some big signal boxes had huge frames of interlocking levers, giving the name 'lever frame' to the rows of levers in a traditional signal box. The levers in a signal box are colour coded: red is for stop signals, yellow for distant signals, black for points, blue for point locks and white for spare levers. Each one has a label, saying clearly what it works.

The interior of a traditional signal box.

The earliest railways were not very good at safety. Few people at first understood how fast and dangerous trains could be. Members of the public would walk along the railways as if they were country lanes. Sometimes they would leave things lying on the rails for the next train to crash into, or even fell asleep on the track. Passengers would try to travel on the roof of the carriage, as they were used to doing on stagecoaches. Never mind that they would be knocked off at the first bridge! Passengers in open carriages, if their hats blew off as the train went along, would jump from the carriage to pick them up. Even if the high-speed fall did not kill them, they would have no chance of catching up with the train again.

Railway staff were in equal danger, and working on the early steam railways could be one of the most dangerous jobs to have. In a single year – 1900 – over 16,000 railway workers were killed or injured. By 1913, this number rose to 30,000. Demands from the trades unions and threats of new laws from the government made the railway companies take safety more seriously. Before then, the railway companies had produced rules and regulations, but they were more to do with the safety of customers (who might want compensation if they were injured) and avoiding damage to railway property, rather than the safety of railway workers.

When the railways first started, the government's policy was to let the railway companies run them as they wished. There were almost no rules. Early in the railway age, an accident happened that made the government think again. It was early in the morning of Christmas Eve 1841 and the Great Western Railway had just opened. Near Reading, the railway goes through a deep cutting at Sonning. Heavy rain had caused a landslip, blocking the line with mud. A third-class train was approaching the cutting. In those days, 'third-class' travel meant just open wagons, mixed in with loaded goods wagons. The train crashed into the mud and the passenger wagons crashed into the locomotive. Then the passenger wagons were crushed by all the heavy goods wagons behind them. Eight passengers were killed.

It was a scandal, and it led to the government passing the 1844 Railway Regulation Act, described elsewhere in the book. This was the first of many railway laws passed by the government in the time of Queen Victoria. They were aimed at making the railways more comfortable and safer, and the companies more responsible for what they did. Many of them were opposed by the railway companies because they cost them money.

PICTURE GALLERY

NAMED SERVICES

Some railway companies gave their best services names and glamorous publicity:

Above: The *Coronation* was a streamlined express service, run by the LNER between London King's Cross and Edinburgh. It was launched in 1937, the year of King George VI's coronation, and Gresley's A4 Pacifics, including the famous *Mallard*, used to haul it. One of the features of the service was its observation cars. It is not to be confused with the *Coronation Scot*, another streamlined express service to Scotland, also launched in 1937. This one ran from London Euston to Glasgow along the West Coast Main Line, and was operated by the London Midland & Scottish Railway.

Previous: The French railway launched a luxury service called the *Fleche D'Or* (it means *Golden Arrow*) between Paris and Calais in 1926. Three years later the Southern Railway started a luxury boat train service – also called the *Golden Arrow* – from London to Dover and across the English Channel to link with the *Fleche D'Or*. At the start, it was first-class only, but in the depressed years of the 1930s, there were not enough first-class passengers. From 1931 they added third-class coaches. The service was stopped during the Second World War, but then continued until 1972. It was steam-hauled until 1961.

LMS "ROYAL SCOT" LEAVES EUSTON
BY
NORMAN WILKINSON, R.I.

Above: The *Royal Scot* ran along the West Coast Main Line from London Euston to Glasgow Central. This named service first ran in 1862. Over the years, the trains got heavier and heavier and needed more and more powerful locomotives to pull them. From 1927 to 1933 this job fell to the Royal Scot class 4-6-0 locomotives, one of which is shown in this picture. The named service ended in 2003 but steam haulage was phased out before that, in the 1960s.

Right: The *Bournemouth Belle* was a luxury service between London Waterloo and Bournemouth. It was operated by the Southern Railway (and later by British Railways) from 1931 to 1967. Early on they changed the service to stop at Southampton and pick up ferry and cruise ship passengers, including many famous people. Before the war, it was hauled by Lord Nelson Class locomotives, and afterwards by the Merchant Navy Class. It was steam-hauled almost until the end of its life.

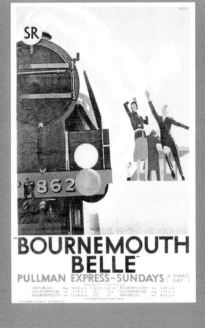

"BOURNEMOUTH BELLE"
PULLMAN EXPRESS—SUNDAYS (& XMAS DAY)

CHAPTER 9

PEOPLE CARRIERS – PASSENGER RAILWAYS

Most of the first railways were built mainly to carry goods, not people. The Stockton & Darlington railway was mainly for coal; for the Liverpool & Manchester it was cotton and cotton cloth; and for the Great Western it was goods arriving by ship at the port of Bristol, going to their main market in London. The early railway companies were often surprised to find how many passengers wanted to travel on their lines. They were also surprised that passenger traffic could be more profitable than carrying freight. The Liverpool & Manchester railway had to delay the start of goods deliveries until they got more trains, so great was the demand from passengers.

Part of the reason for there being so many passengers was first that the railways quickly put all the stagecoach competition out of business; secondly they were much cheaper than the stagecoaches, so more people than before could now afford to travel; and thirdly they were much quicker, making new types of journey possible (for example, businessmen could now do return day trips between Manchester and Liverpool, something that was not practicable in a stagecoach). Having said this, railways did differ in their number of passengers. Some lines, such as London to Brighton, carried mostly passengers, while others (such as those in South Wales) carried mostly goods (in their case, coal).

It could be more expensive for the railways to carry passengers than goods, because passengers needed things like waiting rooms, toilets, refreshment rooms and ticket offices. Goods needed little more than a shed. Passenger carriages were also more expensive than goods wagons (apart from some of the third-class carriages). But not all passengers' requirements were the same.

One of the first-class carriages used on the Liverpool & Manchester Railway in 1838. Its links back to the old horse-drawn stagecoaches are clear.

Some of the earliest passenger carriages looked very like the stagecoaches they replaced. This was partly because they were usually made by the same people. The early ones had almost entirely wooden bodies and were often beautifully (and expensively) painted. There were racks on the roof to carry their luggage but, unlike the stagecoaches, passengers were not supposed to ride on the roof.

In the stagecoach days before railways, passengers could choose how to travel. People who were very rich might have their own private carriage to ride in, or their own horse to ride. The slightly less rich had the stagecoach, where they had the choice of travelling inside or outside of the stagecoach. Poorer people might have to walk, or get a lift on a goods wagon that was no faster than walking.

Come the railway and, as we saw, passengers again had choices. The very rich could have their private carriage put onto a special railway wagon, so they could travel without having anything to do with the other passengers. Next were first-class passengers, who could travel in carriages rather like stagecoaches, protected from the weather. The second-class passenger might have a carriage with a roof, but with no padded seats and no glass in the windows. So the passengers still might get cold and wet, but at least their journeys were quicker and cheaper than by stagecoach, and they had a bit more shelter than the outdoor stagecoach passengers.

The poor third-class travellers might find themselves in an open truck, where the rain and snow fell on them in winter, the sun baked them in summer and the dirt and smoke from the train made them filthy. The only comfort they were given were holes in the wagon floor to let the rain water drain out from around their feet. Travelling third-class could be really dangerous in bad weather. One freezing winter's day, the railway staff on the Great Western found a third-class passenger in his open truck, nearly dead from the cold. Did they help him? No! They lifted him from the train, carried him out of the station and left him in the street outside to die. They did not want to have to deal with a death on railway premises!

The scandal of the Sonning rail crash (described in the chapter on safety) led to the Railway Regulation Act 1844. This made railway companies run at least one service a day in each direction, giving third-class passengers proper seating and full weather protection, charging a fare of no more than

A Great Western second-class 'carriage' of the 1840s – wooden bench seats and a roof – but no glass in the windows.

an old penny a mile and going at a minimum speed of 12 miles an hour. But even this did not bring luxury. The Great Western's idea of 'full weather protection' was a kind of cattle truck, with no windows, no lighting and very little ventilation. Sixty people were crammed onto hard wooden benches in a space of just 6.3 metres by 2.6 metres (about 20 feet, 6 inches by 8 feet, 6 inches). Third-class travel did not become comfortable until later in the nineteenth century.

Some railways deliberately made conditions bad for third-class travellers. They were afraid that, if they made third-class too comfortable, their second-class customers would move to third-class and the railway would lose money. The Glasgow Paisley Kilmarnock & Ayr Railway provided third-class carriages that did not have any seats in them, and the Sheffield Ashton & Manchester Railway even had wagons that could be used either by cattle or by human beings.

Fortunately, not everyone thought that way. The General Manager of the Midland Railway, James Allport, had travelled in America and was very impressed by the standard of carriages provided by the American railwayman George Pullman. So in 1875 the Midland scrapped second class altogether and made their third-class carriages at least as good as the old second-class ones. It sounded like a mad business idea but it worked. Profits went up and, one by one, the other companies were forced to do the same. The last changeover by a railway company to a two-class system was in 1938. By 1888, 88 per cent of national ticket sales were for third-class tickets. The railways continued to have just first- and third-class carriages until 1956, when 'third-class' was re-named 'standard class'.

It might not be the luxury carriages for which you paid extra, it might be the speed of the service. Railways started introducing higher-priced, fast express services in the 1840s. But these were not very popular. They started to be phased out in 1859 and were mostly gone by 1890.

One important difference between many Victorian carriages and modern ones was that many Victorian carriages were divided into small compartments, and there was no corridor between one part of the train and another. These types of trains could not provide toilets or dining cars; you had to wait until the train reached a station, leap out, get something to eat or drink, or visit the toilet, and hope you would get back to your compartment before the train left. Worse still, if someone odd or scary

A Great Western third-class 'carriage' of the 1840s – actually just an open truck with bench seats.

got into the compartment with you, you were stuck with them until the next station. You could not move to another part of the train. To deal with this, railways started providing an emergency cord, which would ring a bell in the guard's compartment if you pulled it. He would come to see what was wrong once the train was stopped. The first of these was provided by the London & South Western Railway in 1865. Some of the early ones were outside the compartment, so you had to let down the window and lean out to pull it. This was itself dangerous. The modern type of emergency cord, one that stops the train immediately, was not approved until 1893.

Gradually carriages with corridors became more common (the first ones to have corridors throughout were provided by the Great Western in 1892). Corridors meant trains could now have toilets (these became quite common, especially on long-distance services, by the 1890s). The Great Northern Railway provided the first real dining car on their service between London and Leeds in 1879 (but the first dining service that would serve third-class

The ultimate in luxury – Her Majesty's Day Compartment on the London & North Western Railway.

passengers did not appear until 1891). Some early dining cars did not have corridors to connect them to the rest of the train. People wanting to eat on the train had to wait until it was stopped in the station before they could go into the dining car. Nor could they leave it after their meal until the train stopped.

Lighting from the 1840s (if your carriage had any) was by dim and smelly oil lamps. Then in 1863 the North London Railway started providing gas lights. The first electric carriage lighting appeared in 1881, and was provided in all new carriages after 1918, though gas lighting did not disappear from railway carriages completely until the early 1950s.

Sleeping carriages first appeared in 1839 in the United States, where long railway journeys could last for days (and nights). A primitive form of sleeping car, called a bed carriage, was tried in Britain at about the same time and a number of British railways introduced something more like modern sleeping accommodation in the 1870s. At first, sleeping accommodation was limited to first-class passengers but, in 1928, the LMS, LNER and Great Western laid on sleeping accommodation for the third-class traveller. But there was no luxury for them. They simply got to hire a rug and a pillow, and had to provide their own bed linen.

The demand for sleeping accommodation was always limited on an island as small as Britain and competition from aeroplanes and from cars and coaches on motorways took away much of that trade in recent years. In 1900 there were six overnight sleepers running to Scotland alone. By 2014 there were only two sleeper services in the whole of the United Kingdom.

Few carriages had heating until the 1890s. Before then, you could hire foot warmers – a kind of hot water bottle – from platform staff. The Midland Railway possessed 27,000 of these in 1905. Carriage heating was developed from the 1890s using steam from the locomotive (electric trains had electric heaters and many post-war diesel engines had separate boilers for making steam to heat the carriages). Today's British Railways trains have electric heating. The big change in carriages in the twentieth century came from 1964 onwards. Up to then, carriages tended to have separate compartments and a corridor along one side. The new ones had an open coach with a passageway through the middle of the carriage. They also had improved

Even more luxury – the twelve-wheeled carriages of the Royal saloons, built for King Edward VII in 1903.

suspension. The most modern luxury, air conditioning, was tried out in a couple of Great Western dining cars in 1935, but did not start to appear in ordinary carriages until 1971. This new comfort helped to stop unhappy travellers moving away from the railway.

Most of these improvements meant a lot of extra weight for the locomotive to haul, but added nothing to the number of passengers a train could carry. A corridor took out two seats from each compartment, and a restaurant car was expensive to build, heavy to pull and needed extra staff, but did not seat a single extra passenger. On a full train in the 1890s, for every passenger 1.25 tons of rolling stock had to be pulled. Ever bigger and more powerful locomotives were needed.

One thing the railways invented was the ticket. In the stagecoach and early railway days, tickets were handwritten and then torn out of a book (which is why even today we talk about 'booking a ticket'). The first railways often sold their tickets at a nearby hotel or pub but, as they got permanent stations, they provided their own ticket offices. Some big stations might have a confusing number of different ticket offices, depending upon what class you were travelling, what railway company you were travelling with or where you were going.

A man named Thomas Edmondson, a stationmaster on the Newcastle & Carlisle Railway, invented a system for printing and numbering tickets. This made it easier to keep a record of how many tickets had been sold and how much money collected. His system was used by the railway from the 1840s to 1990.

The earliest carriages were little bigger than the stagecoaches they replaced. They were joined together by chains and had buffers without springs in them, all of which would have given a very uncomfortable, jerky ride. Over the years, the carriages became much longer and were beginning to run on eight or twelve wheels, rather than four or six, and had spring buffers, all of which made for a smoother ride. They were also made safer – after a series of train fires in the years before and during the First World War, they were made a lot more fire-proof. By 1914 the roof, body panelling and underframes of new coaches would normally be in steel, while electricity was replacing gas as the means of lighting.

But the uncomfortable old six-wheeler carriages remained in service on some British suburban lines until well into the twentieth century. There they faced competition from the trams, and the Steam Rail Motor (described elsewhere in the book) was developed by the railways to take them on.

The steam railways also joined up with other long-distance ways of travelling. From the earliest days Brunel had plans for a Great Western service between London and New York, using the steam ships he designed to cross the Atlantic. In the speed records part of the book we saw how the railways used to meet up with the ocean liners as they landed at Plymouth. In 1939 a train from Victoria would take you to Southampton to catch one of the Empire flying boats going to far-off parts of the world. For a time before the Second World War the railway companies even had their own airline.

Slip coaches were one feature of passenger railways in the steam days that we do not see today. A slip coach was one that could be detached from the back of a moving train. If a train service wanted to drop passengers off at stations along the line, but did not want the delay of stopping at the station, they could attach one or more slip coaches to the back of the train. As they got near the station, a special guard would uncouple the coach. As the rest of the train disappeared into the distance, the slip coach would roll

A trainload of passengers pulls out of Bridgnorth station on the Severn Valley Railway.

into the station, where the guard would put on its brakes to stop it at the platform. There, the passengers could either get out, or their carriage could be attached to a branch-line train. Up to three slip coaches were used on some services.

The first slip coach was used as early as 1840 on the (cable-hauled) London & Blackwall Railway. Their first use on a steam railway was by the London Brighton & South Coast Railway. In 1858 they slipped the Lewes part of the Brighton express at Haywards Heath. By 1914 there were 200 slip coach services in use, seventy-two of them on the Great Western Railway. But by the end of the First World War the number of Great Western 'slips' was down to seventeen. The last slip coach service (at Bicester) was stopped in 1960. They fell out of fashion: (a) because an extra member of staff had to be employed to work each one; (b) no one ever worked out a way of picking up the slipped coaches on the return journey without stopping the train and (c) some passengers were nervous about them.

CHAPTER 10

FREIGHT AND FREIGHT WAGONS

The railways moved raw materials and manufactured goods around more quickly and cheaply than ever before. This helped the Industrial Revolution to take place. They also changed the lives of city dwellers. For the first time, enough food and fuel could be brought into the cities to feed and warm their growing populations. People's diets also improved, since more fresh food could now be delivered to the cities.

In the days before steam engines, most railways were for carrying coal (or other minerals). They had two main types of wagons. The first was called the chaldron, which carried the coal. A chaldron is a measure of weight – just over 2.5 tons. The other type of wagon was a flat truck, which carried anything that could be tied onto it and covered with a tarpaulin to protect it from sparks. A third type of truck soon came into use, with sides high enough to hold its cargo in securely.

Early railways had different rules for the wagons that ran on their lines. Some railways owned no wagons at all and let the users of the line provide their own. Others provided wagons and rented them out to their customers. Most railways would accept wagons provided by private railway users, but these were sometimes badly designed, badly built and badly maintained. One lot of private owners' wagons might not even be able to connect up with another lot. Private owners' wagons became a menace for some railways. The railways tried at least to get them made to a standard design, but they were not always successful. Only in the 1890s were national standards for wagons set out and new private wagons tested to make sure they were up to standard.

Many of the wagons on the railways were owned by private companies, and they were not always as well maintained as they should have been.

Nor were there at first any national rules about what the loading gauge for railways should be. Each railway made up the rules to suit their local needs, and other trains with a bigger loading gauge ran the risk of crashing into things like bridges, tunnels or platforms.

New types of wagons were introduced. There were covered wagons for goods that needed to be protected from the weather; longer wagons, ones that ran on bogies; double-decker wagons for carrying sheep, and all sorts of specialist wagons for carrying everything from bananas to gunpowder to dead bodies. Some railway companies tried to bring in much larger wagons to save money, but it was sometimes hard to find loads big enough to fill them. Tank wagons to carry liquids first appeared in 1865, but did not become common until the mid-1880s. Before that, milk, for example, had to be transported in churns holding a few gallons; other liquids went in barrels. The new milk wagons carried thousands of gallons of milk in glass-lined tankers.

All these different types of wagons were difficult to list in telegraph messages, so railway staff invented short nicknames for them. So for

Milk wagon: This wagon was built to transport churns of milk in the days before tank wagons. It has doors along the side that can be opened as the train goes along, letting in a breeze to keep the milk cool and fresh.

example the brake van, where the guard sat, was called a 'toad'; covered goods wagons were 'minks'; tank wagons were 'cordons'; fish wagons 'tadpoles'; flat wagons 'beavers'; and meat vans 'micas'.

Having lots of small wagons carrying different things was very inefficient. It took ages to move all the wagons around and attach them all to the right train, so that they all got to the right place. This was called shunting, and often took place in a huge area of tracks called a marshalling yard. Someone worked out that, for every 100 miles a freight train covered, it took 75 miles-worth of shunting to put the train together. Modern freight services tend to have fewer, larger wagons, with lots of them carrying the same goods. They often carry bulk goods, like sand, stones or coal – the kind of jobs railways are best at.

In the days when almost everything was transported by rail, the railways had a legal duty to be a **common carrier**. That is, they were required by law to transport any goods a customer might want moving, from anywhere to anywhere, at a price set by the government. This could mean transporting loads that were not profitable. As road transport began to compete more with rail, the same requirement was not put on the road hauliers. That meant they could compete for the railways' profitable work by offering cheaper rates, but leave the railways to deal with the unprofitable deliveries. This common carrier rule was not scrapped until 1953.

The railways' work did not stop when the goods reached the station. They had horses and carts to deliver the parcels to people's homes and businesses. From 1948, these started to be replaced by 'mechanical horses' – little three-wheeler Scammel Scarab lorries.

Passenger trains had introduced continuous brakes on all the carriages early on, but early goods trains had brakes only on the engine itself and in the guard's van. It took them a long time to stop, so most goods trains could only travel very slowly – often about 20 miles an hour. These used to hold up all the other trains using the line, and the problem got worse as the passenger trains got faster. However, private owners could not – or would not – find the money to put continuous brakes on the wagons they owned.

Gunpowder wagon – these wagons had to be protected from sparks from the engine.

Grain wagon.

Even the railways found it very expensive to do it on their own wagons. The Great Western finally started putting brakes on their wagons in 1903 and other major companies followed them. Still, when the railways were taken over by the government in 1948 they still had to scrap two out of every five privately owned wagons.

The railways only really started to deal with the brakes problem in the 1955 Modernisation Plan. This set aside £75 million (a lot of money today, but an even bigger sum in 1955) to fit brakes to its goods wagons. By 1959 almost a third of British Railways' 945,250 goods wagons had continuous brakes. But the Modernisation Plan got a lot of things wrong about freight. It ordered far more new wagons than it really needed. Between 1948 and 1958 they ordered an average of 30,000 new wagons a year. Nevertheless, the end of the common carrier rule, the reduction in coal deliveries and competition from road transport all reduced demand. By 1964 the year's orders for new wagons had fallen to just 769.

The guard's van. On early freight trains, this and the locomotive itself would be the only part of the train with any brakes.

Above: During the Second World War, almost everything was transported by rail. This truck is a replica of one carrying a propeller for a Royal Air Force aircraft.

Opposite bottom: Banana wagon – these wagons had to be heated.

Travelling post offices

From their earliest days, the railways helped to deliver mail. The postal service had an agreement with the Liverpool & Manchester Railway in 1830 and, by 1838, there was an Act of Parliament that said that all railways had to do the same. At first, it just meant putting the horse-drawn mail coaches on a wagon, making part of their journey by rail. But, also in 1838, the Grand Junction Railway tried sorting the mail while it was travelling, using a converted horsebox. This was the first travelling post office, or TPO.

At first, the only way of delivering the bags of sorted mail was a dangerous one – they would throw them onto the platform as the train passed through the station. But soon they developed devices along the track to pick up and drop off mail. The mail sack being dropped off was hung out of the side of the TPO carriage and caught in a net at the side of the track. The mail sack

Mail pick-up and drop-off – the trackside equipment.

A Travelling Post Office mail coach, with its net for catching trackside mail bags.

to be picked up was hung on a pole beside the track and scooped up by a net hung from the side of the TPO carriage.

Conditions in the early TPOs were bad for the post office workers. The carriages swayed about as they tried to work, the fumes from the oil lamps gave them headaches, and there was no heating or toilet in them. Even so, the staff used to sort 2,000 letters an hour with 99 per cent accuracy.

TPOs became big business for the railways. The biggest ones had six sorting carriages, eleven carriages for storing mail and fifty staff. Nor were the mail trains slow. The *City of Truro* was doing a mail delivery in 1904 when it became the first train to record a speed of 100 miles an hour. TPOs also became big business for criminals one night in 1963. Thieves held up a mail train in Buckinghamshire and stole £2.3 million in what became known as the Great Train Robbery.

The Post Office stopped using railway Travelling Post Offices in 2004.

The railways did two other important things for communications in the nineteenth century. The first involved newspapers. Before the railways, there were no real national newspapers, because they could not be delivered in time for the news to be fresh. With the railways, newspapers printed in London were on sale at the far ends of the country the same day. People could be much better informed about what was going on in the world.

The second thing was the electric telegraph. The telegraph was the email of the nineteenth century. It could send messages from one end of the country to the other in seconds. The railways were some of the first businesses to use it, and the railway lines provided the ideal route for the telegraph wires that carried the messages. By the 1870s, Britain had 87,000 miles of telegraph line and 5,179 telegraph offices. Many of those offices were in railway stations, and many of those miles of telegraph line ran alongside railway tracks. People could now send instructions, questions, news – any kind of message – in an instant.

PICTURE GALLERY

AROUND THE STATION

From 1848, W.H. Smith made his fortune by opening shops selling newspapers, magazines and books at just about every railway station in the country.

Railwaymen used to take great pride in the gardens on their station platforms, a tradition carried on here at Ropley on the Mid-Hants Railway.

Steam railways are keen to attract younger visitors. Here the Kent & East Sussex Railway receive a visit from Thomas the Tank Engine.

CHAPTER 11

WHERE TO FIND STEAM RAILWAYS

We are lucky in the British Isles in the number of steam railways we have saved. But how do you find out about the ones near where you live, or near to places you are visiting? If you search for 'British steam railways' on the internet, you will find a lot of useful sites. One site I find helpful is www.heritage-railways.com. This will give you a map of the British Isles, showing all the preserved railways as dots. Just click on any of the dots and it will give you information about that railway. You can then find out more from that railway's own website.

I have looked here at just a few of them. I chose them not because they were the biggest and best (though some may well be), but so that all the different parts of the country were included.

The Bodmin & Wenford Railway: A 13-mile round trip from Bodmin General station on Cornwall's only full-sized steam railway. It shows you what a Great Western Cornish branch line of the 1950s was like. Visit www.bodminrailway.co.uk.

The West Somerset Railway: Britain's longest heritage steam railway, giving a 40-mile round trip between Bishops Lydeard (4 miles from Taunton) and Minehead. The route takes in the Quantock Hills and the Somerset coast. The station at Minehead is right opposite the beach. Visit www.west-somerset-railway.co.uk.

The Avon Valley Railway: Currently providing a 6-mile round trip, starting from Oldland Common, going through the restored Midland Railway station at Bitton, near Bristol, and serving the Avon Valley Country Park, giving connections to boat trips. There are plans to extend it to Bath. Visit www.avonvalleyrailway.org.

Fascination with steam travel is not just limited to the railways.

Steam – the Museum of the Great Western Railway: Based in the old railway works in the middle of Swindon, the museum tells the story of the Great Western Railway and its creator, Isambard Kingdom Brunel. There are no live steam engines, but lots of history and things to do. Visit www.steam-museum.org.uk.

Didcot Railway Centre: A working museum of the Great Western Railway, located next door to Didcot main-line station and based on the 1930s engine shed. A half-mile demonstration line, a short branch line and one of the biggest collections of locomotives, including replicas of 1840s broad-gauge engines and the historically important Edwardian Steam Rail Motor. Visit www.didcotrailwaycentre.org.uk.

The Mid-Hants Railway (the Watercress Line): A 20-mile round trip through attractive countryside between the market towns of Alton and Alresford in Hampshire. Visit www.watercressline.co.uk.

The Bluebell Railway: Britain's first full-sized preserved steam railway, part of the old London, Brighton & South Coast Railway, reopened in 1960. It runs for a 22-mile round trip along the border of East and West Sussex, between Sheffield Park and East Grinstead. Visit www.bluebell-railway.co.uk.

The Kent & East Sussex Railway: A 21-mile round trip through the Rother Valley from Tenterden to Bodiham, with its wonderful ancient castle. Visit www.kesr.org.uk.

Romney Hythe & Dymchurch Railway: A narrow-gauge (15 inch) railway, giving a 27-mile round trip between Hythe (near the Channel Tunnel) and the remarkable seaside landscape at Dungeness. It was opened in 1927 as 'the world's smallest public railway' and was turned into an armoured military train during the war to guard against a German invasion. Visit www.rhdr.org.uk.

No. 60163 *Tornado*: The first of the post-steam age steam locomotives.

North Norfolk Railway: Part of the former Midland & Great Northern Joint Railway, running from Sheringham to Holt. The 11-mile round trip offers views of the Norfolk coast and countryside. Visit www.nnrailway.co.uk.

Nene Valley Railway: A 15-mile round trip between Peterborough city centre and a site near the East Coast Main Line, passing through the water meadows, country park and farmland of the Nene Valley. The railway has been used as a location for some of the James Bond films. Visit www.nvr.org.uk.

Great Central Railway: Originally part of the main line between Sheffield and London, this preserved railway now provides a 16-mile round trip between Loughborough and Leicester. It is the country's only double-tracked main-line heritage railway. Visit www.gcr.co.uk.

Severn Valley Railway: A 32-mile round trip through the attractive scenery of the Severn Valley, between Kidderminster and Bridgnorth. There is a visitor centre at Highley, midway along the route. Visit www.svr.co.uk.

A handcart that railway workers can use to travel along the tracks without a locomotive, working the seesaw lever on top.

A police station. In the earliest days, the railways would have had a policeman stationed at about one-mile intervals along the track to act as human railway signals. A hut like this – or a police station as it was called – was their only protection against the weather.

Talyllyn Railway: A narrow-gauge (2 foot, 3 inch) railway, based at Tywyn in Gwynedd, it offers a 15-mile round trip through the scenery of mid-Wales. It was the world's first steam railway to be preserved (in 1951). Visit www.talyllyn.co.uk.

Festiniog Railway: A narrow-gauge (2 foot) railway with a round trip of 27 miles. Its unusual double-ended locomotives climb over 700 feet from the harbour at Porthmadog, through spectacular scenery in the Snowdonia National Park to the slate-mining town of Blaenau Festiniog. Visit www.festrail.co.uk.

East Lancashire Railway: This line was closed by British Rail in 1982 and reopened by the railway trust in 1987. Running between Rawtenstall and Heywood, the railway offers a 24-mile round trip and also has its own transport museum. It links with the national network at Castleton. Visit www.eastlancsrailway.org.uk.

Keighley & Worth Valley Railway: A branch line, running from Keighley (where it joins the national network) up the Worth Valley to Oxenhope, a 10-mile round trip. The railway has been widely used as a location for films and television programmes. Visit www.kwvr.co.uk.

No. 92212 Class 9F 2-10-0: The Class 9Fs were the last steam engines to be built by British Railways. *Evening Star*, their very last new locomotive, was a 9F. They were some of the most powerful locomotives British Railways ever built (they could pull a 900-ton train at 35 miles an hour). They were also fast (one of them was timed at over 90 miles an hour in 1958). They were also a big waste of money – 251 of them were built, costing up to £34,000 each, and some of them were only in service for five years before being scrapped. This one was built in 1959 and scrapped in 1968. It only covered 78,166 miles for British Railways. Bought by enthusiasts, it was last restored in 2009 and is currently at the Mid-Hants Railway.

National Railway Museum: Based at York and Shildon, the NRM is the world's leading railway museum. It houses such famous steam locomotives as the A4 *Mallard* and the *Flying Scotsman* and attracts almost a million visitors a year. Visit www.nrm.org.uk.

Ravenglass & Eskdale Railway: A 15-inch narrow-gauge railway running from the port of Ravenglass to the foothills of the Lake District, a round trip of 14 miles. Visit www.ravenglass-railway.co.uk.

Strathspey Steam Railway: A 20-mile round trip, starting from Aviemore, along part of the original Highland Railway. Scenic attractions include the River Spey and the Cairngorm mountains. Visit www.strathspeyrailway.co.uk.

The Jacobite: Reckoned to be one of the greatest railway trips in the world, this steam service runs from Fort William, in the shadow of Ben Nevis,

The Lancashire Fusilier, one of eighteen preserved Stanier Black Fives out of the total of 226 originally ordered by the LMS. This one was built in 1937 and withdrawn from service in August 1968. Enthusiasts bought it for £3,300 and restored it. It is seen here hauling the Jacobite service through the Scottish Highlands.

Britain's tallest mountain, to the fishing and ferry port of Mallaig. An 84-mile round trip through spectacular scenery, it was used for the railway parts of the Harry Potter films, among others. This is a steam rail service, but not a preserved railway. It is run on the national rail network under licence. Visit www.westcoastrailways.co.uk/jacobite.

Railway Preservation Society of Ireland: Based at Whitehead, County Antrim and operating on the Irish standard gauge of 5 feet, 3 inches, the Society is described as the premier preserved railway in Ireland. Visit www.steamtrainsireland.com.

ACKNOWLEDGEMENTS

Many people have helped me with this book. My particular thanks go to Dave Beeley and Richard Jones of the Education team at Didcot Railway Centre for their helpful editorial suggestions and technical advice, to Richard Preston and Ian Payne, and to my son Michael for his help with the diagrams. Any errors or omissions which remain in the book are my responsibility entirely. I have tried not to use any illustrations in the book that may be subject to copyright. If I have failed in any particular, please let me know via the publisher. If I, and the book, survive to a second edition, I will try to ensure that any shortcomings are corrected. Unless a caption says otherwise, the pictures are taken by me or come from my own collection.